بسم الله الرحمن الرحيم

تزكية النفوس

و تربيتها
كما يقرره علماء السلف

إبن رجب الحنبلي   إبن القيم الجوزية   أبو حامد الغزالي

THE PURIFICATION
OF THE SOUL

according to the earliest sources

compiled from the works of
Ibn Rajab al-Hanbali, Ibn al-Qayyim al-Jawziyya,
and Abu Hamid al-Ghazali

collected and arranged by
Ahmad Farid

Al-Firdous Ltd, London

1991 : First Edition.
1993 : Second Revised Edition.
1995 : Third Edition.
1996 : Reprinted
1998 : Reprinted

Translated from the Arabic by Ashraf.

Revised by al-'Arabi Ben Razzuq and Ahmad Thomson.

Typeset by Omar Johnstone and Ahmad Thomson

The English translations of the Qur'an appearing in the text are based on that o Pick of Muhammad Pickthall, *alehi rahma.*

Originally published in Arabic as *Tazkiyat an-Nufus wa Tarbiyyatuha kama Yuqarriruhu 'Ulama' as-Salaf,* Dar al- Qalam, Beirut, Lebanon (undated).

ISBN 1 874263 00 0

Available from   and from

Al-Firdous Ltd
10 Fonthill Road
London N4 3HX
Tel: 0171 564 6896

Ta-Ha Publishers Ltd.
1 Wynne Road
London SW9 0BB
Tel: 0171 737 7266
website:http://www.taha.co.uk/
email: sales@taha.co.uk

Printed and Bound by- De-Luxe Printers, London NW10 7NR.
website: http://www.de-luxe.com email: printers@de-luxe.com

CONTENTS

Author's Preface

إن الحمد لله نحمده ونستعينه ونستغفره ونعوذ بالله من شرور أنفسنا
وسيئات أعمالنا ، من يهده فلا مضلٌ له ومن يضلل فلا هادي له، ونشهد أن
لا إله إلا الله وحده لا شريك له ونشهد ان محمداً عبده ورسوله – صلى اللهم
عليه وعلى آله وصحبه وسلم

All praise is for Allah. We praise Him and seek His
assistance. We ask for His forgiveness and take refuge in
Him from the evil within ourselves and from the evil of
our deeds. He whom Allah guides will never be diverted
yet whomever He sends astray will never find his way. I
bear witness that there is no god but Allah, alone, He has
no partner, and I bear witness that Muhammed is His
servant and messenger, may Your blessings and peace be
on him and on his family and on his companions.

One of the most important tasks for which the Prophet
of this nation, Muhammed ﷺ, was sent was the purification of the soul. Allah says, speaking of this mission,

❴ It is He who sent to an illiterate people a messenger
from amongst themselves, reciting to them His signs
and purifying them and teaching them the Book and
the wisdom even though before they were clearly in
error. (62:2) ❵

So whoever truly hopes for Allah and the Last Day
should have a special interest in the purification of his
own soul, for Allah has linked the success of His servant
with the purity of his soul, after making eleven consecu-

tive oaths. There is not to be found in the Qur'an another oath such as this. Allah says:

> ❨ By the sun and his brightness, and the moon when she follows him, and the day when it reveals him, and the night when it enshrouds him, and the heaven and Him Who built it, And the earth and Him Who spread it out, and a soul and Him Who perfected it and inspired it with awareness of what is wrong for it and what is right for it, he is indeed successful who purifies it, and he is indeed a failure who neglects it. (91:1-10) ❩

The word *tazkiat* means to purify or to cleanse; the word *zakat* comes from the same root, since *zakat* purifies wealth by the recognition of Allah's right over a portion of it.

It has now become difficult for us to benefit directly from the books of *raqa'iq* (books on subjects which affect the emotions) written by the first generations of Muslim scholars. Most of these are large books comprising many volumes and are difficult for most Muslims to have access to; in addition to this they frequently contain weak and fabricated reports. Thus we have set out to compile a collection of the most reliable reports which have come to us from some of the scholars whose expertise lay in the field of *dawa: Imam* Shamsudin ibn al-Qayyim, Ibn Rajab al-Hanbali, and *Imam* Abu Hamid al-Ghazali. It is our sincere desire that this book will be a useful resource and ultimately prove to be of benefit on that Day when neither money nor children will be of benefit, for none will benefit except for those who come with a pure heart.

All Praise is for Allah and all Power is His.
He is our Lord and to Him is the end of all journeys

ONE

SINCERITY

Sincerity is the freeing of one's intentions from all impurities in order to come nearer to Allah. It is to ensure that the intentions behind all acts of worship and obedience to Allah are exclusively for His pleasure. It is the perpetual contemplation of the Creator, to the extent that one forgets the creation.

Sincerity is a condition for Allah's acceptance of good deeds performed in accordance with the *sunnah* of the Prophet, may Allah bless him and grant him peace. Allah has commanded this in the Qur'an:

❴ And they have been commanded to worship only Allah, being sincere towards Him in their *deen* and true. (98:5) ❵

Abu Umama has related that a man once came to the Prophet, may Allah bless him and grant him peace, and said, "What of a man who joined us in the fighting, his intention being for fame and booty?" The Prophet said, "He receives nothing." The man repeated the question three times and each time the Prophet said, "He receives nothing". Then he said, "Allah only accepts actions that are intended purely for His pleasure." [1]

Abu Sa'id al-Khudri related that the Prophet ﷺ said in his *khutbah* during the farewell pilgrimage, "Allah will

bless whoever hears these words and whoever under-
stands them, for it may be that those who pass on this
knowledge are not those who will understand it the best.
There are three things concerning which the heart of a believer should feel no enmity or malice: devoting one's actions to Allah, giving counsel to the *Imams* of the Muslims,
and being loyal to the majority." [2]

What is meant here is that these three things strengthen
the heart, and whoever distinguishes himself in them will
have a heart purified from all manner of deceit, corruption
and evil.

A servant can only free himself from *shaytan* through
sincere devotion, for Allah tells us in the Quran that Iblis
said to Him:

❨ Except those of Your servants who are sincere.
(38:83) ❩

It has been related that a righteous man used to say, "O
self, be devout and you will be pure." When any worldly
fortune, in which the self finds comfort and towards which
the heart inclines, intrudes upon our worship, then it im-
pairs the purity of our efforts and ruins our sincerity. Man
is preoccupied with his good fortune and immersed in his
desires and appetites; rarely are his actions or acts of worship free of temporary objectives and desires of this kind.
For this reason it has been said that whoever secures a single moment of pure devotion to Allah in his life will survive, for devotion is rare and precious, and cleansing the
heart of its impurities is an exacting undertaking.

In fact, devotion is the purifying of the heart from all
impurities, whether few or many, so that the intention of
drawing nearer to Allah is freed from all other motives, except that of seeking His pleasure. This can only come from

a lover of Allah, who is so absorbed in contemplation of the next world that there remains in his heart no place for the love of this world. Such a person must be devout and pure in all his actions, even in eating, drinking and answering the calls of nature. With rare exceptions, anyone who is not like this will find the door of devotion closed in his face.

The everyday actions of a person who is overwhelmed by his or her love for Allah and the *akhira* are characterised by this love and they are, in fact, pure devotion. In the same way, anyone whose soul is overwhelmed by love for and preoccupation with this world, or status and authority, will be so overwhelmed by these things that no act of worship, be it prayer or fasting, will be acceptable, except in very rare cases.

The remedy for love of this world is to break the worldly desires of the self, ending its greed for this world and purifying it in preparation for the next world. This will then become the state of the heart and sincere devotion will become easier to attain. There are a great many actions where a man acts, thinking they are purely intended for Allah's pleasure, but he is deluded, for he fails to see the defects in them.

It has been related that a man was used to praying in the first row in the mosque. One day he was late for the prayer, so he prayed in the second row. Feeling embarrassment when people saw him in the second row, he realised that the pleasure and satisfaction of the heart that he used to gain from praying in the first row were due to his seeing people seeing him there and admiring him for it. This is a subtle and intangible condition and actions are rarely safe from it. Apart from those whom Allah has assisted, few are aware of such delicate matters. Those who do not realise it only come to see their good deeds appearing as bad ones on the Day of Resurrection; they are the ones referred to in Allah's words:

❨ And something will come to them from Allah which they had never anticipated, for the evil of their deeds will become apparent to them. (39:47-48) ❩

And also:

❨ Say: Shall We tell you who will lose most in respect of their deeds? Those whose efforts were astray in the life of this world, while they thought that they were doing good works. (18:103-104) ❩

Yaqub said: "A devout person is someone who conceals things that are good, in the same way that he conceals things that are bad."

As-Sousi said: "True devotion is to lose the faculty of being conscious of your devotion; for someone who identifies devotion in his devotion is a person whose devotion is in need of devotion." To contemplate devotion is to admire it, and admiration is an affliction; and that which is pure is whatever is free of all afflictions. This means that one's deeds should be purified from any self-admiration concerning the actions they entail.

Ayyub said: "It is much harder for the people of action to purify their intentions than it is to execute any of their actions."

Some people have said: "To be devout for a short while is to survive for ever, but devotion is rare."

Suhail was asked: "What is the most difficult thing for the self?" He said: "Devotion, when the self does not have the good fortune of being endowed with it."

Al-Fudayl said: "Forsaking action for the sake of other

people is to seek their admiration. To act for the sake of their admiration is to associate others with Allah. Devotion is when Allah frees you from both of these states."

Notes

1. *Sahih*, an-Nisa'i, *Kitab al-Jihad*, 6/25; al-Hafidh ibn Hajar, *Fath al-Qadir*, 6/28.
2. *Sahih*, Ibn Ma'jah; also Ibn Hibban, *Mawarid adh-Dham'an*, p. 47, on the authority of Zaid ibn Thabit.

TWO

THE NATURE OF INTENTION

The intention of a person is not his utterance of the words, "I intend to do so and so." It is an overflowing from the heart which runs like conquests inspired by Allah. At times it is made easy, at other times, difficult. A person whose heart is overwhelmingly righteous finds it easy to summon good intentions at most times. Such a person has a heart generally inclined to the roots of goodness which, most of the time, blossom into the manifestation of good actions. As for those whose hearts incline towards and are overwhelmed by worldly matters, they find this difficult to accomplish and even obligatory acts of worship may become difficult and tiresome.

The Prophet ﷺ said: "Actions are only by intention, and every man shall only have what he intended. Thus he whose *hijra* was for Allah and His Messenger, his *hijra* was for Allah and His Messenger, and he whose *hijra* was to achieve some worldly benefit or to take some woman in marriage, his *hijra* was for that for which he made *hijra*." [1]

Imam ash-Shaf'i said: "This *hadith* is a third of all knowledge." The words, "actions are only by intention", mean that deeds which are performed in accordance with the *sunnah* are only acceptable and rewarded if the intentions behind them were sincere. It is like the saying of the the Prophet, may Allah bless him and grant him peace, "Actions depend upon their outcome." [2]

Likewise, the words, "every man shall only have what he intended", mean that the reward for an action depends upon the intention behind it. After stating this principle, the Prophet ﷺ gave examples of it by saying, "Thus he whose *hijra* was for Allah and His Messenger, his *hijra* was for Allah and His Messenger, and he whose *hijra* was to achieve some worldly benefit or to take some woman in marriage, his *hijra* was for that for which he made *hijra*." So deeds which are apparently identical may differ, because the intentions behind them are different in degrees of goodness and badness, from one person to another.

Good intentions do not change the nature of forbidden actions. The ignorant should not misconstrue the meaning of the *hadith* and think that good intentions could turn forbidden actions into acceptable ones. The above saying of the Prophet ﷺ specifically relates to acts of worship and permissible actions, not to forbidden ones. Worship and permissible actions can be turned into forbidden ones because of the intentions behind them, and permissible actions can become either good or bad deeds by intention; but wrong actions cannot become acts of worship, even with good intentions.³ When bad intentions are accompanied by flaws in the actions themselves, then their gravity and punishment are multiplied.

Any praiseworthy act must be rooted in sound intentions; only then should it be deemed worthy of reward. The fundamental principle should be that the act is intended for the worship of Allah alone. If our intention is to show off, then these same acts of worship will in fact become acts of disobedience. As for permissible deeds, they all involve intentions – which can potentially turn them into excellent acts which bring a man nearer to Allah and confer on him the gift of closeness to Him.

The Excellence of Intention

Umar ibn al-Khattab, may Allah be pleased with him, said: "The best acts are doing what Allah has commanded, staying far away from what Allah has forbidden, and having sincere intentions towards what- ever Allah has required of us."[4]

Some of our predecessors said: "Many small actions are made great by the intentions behind them. Many great actions, on the other hand, are made small because the intentions behind them are lacking."

Yahya Ibn Abu Kathir said: "Learn about intentions, for their importance is greater than the importance of actions."

Ibn Umar once heard a man who was putting on his *ihram* say: "O Allah! I intend to do the *Hajj* and *Umrah*." So he said to him: "Is it not in fact the people whom you are informing of your intentions? Does not Allah already know what is in your heart?"[5] It is because good intentions are exclusively the concern of the heart, that they should not be voiced during worship.

The Excellence of Knowledge and Teaching

There are many proofs in the Qur'an concerning the excellence of knowledge and its transmission. Allah, the Mighty and Glorious, says:

❲ Allah will raise up to high ranks those of you who believe and those who have been given knowledge. (58:11) ❳

And also:

❲ Are those who know equal to those who do not know? (39:9) ❳

Also, in the *hadith*, the Prophet ﷺ says, "When Allah desires good for someone, He gives him understanding of the *deen*."[6] He ﷺ also said, "Allah makes the way to the Garden easy for whoever treads a path in search of knowledge." [7]

Travelling on the path to knowledge refers both to walking along an actual pathway, such as going on foot to the assemblies of the *ulama'*, as well as to following a metaphysical road, such as studying and memorising.

The above saying of the Prophet ﷺ probably means that Allah makes learning the useful knowledge that is sought after easier for the seeker, clearing the way for him and smoothing his journey. Some of our predecessors used to say: "Is there anyone seeking knowledge, so that we can assist him in finding it ?"

This *hadith* also alludes to the road leading to the Garden on the Day of Judgement, which is the straight path – and to what precedes it and what comes after it.

Knowledge is also the shortest path to Allah. Whoever travels the road of knowledge reaches Allah and the Garden by the shortest route. Knowledge also clears the way out of darkness, ignorance, doubt and scepticism. It is why Allah called His Book, "Light".

Al-Bukhari and Muslim have reported on the authority of Abdullah ibn Umar that the Messenger of Allah ﷺ said: "Truly, Allah will not take away knowledge by snatching it away from people, but by taking away the lives of the people of knowledge one by one until none of them survive. Then the people will adopt ignorant ones as their leaders. They will be asked to deliver judgements and they will give them without knowledge, with the result that they will go astray and lead others astray."

When 'Ubadah ibn as-Samit was asked about this *hadith* he said: "If you want, I will tell you what the highest knowledge is, which raises people in rank: it is humility."

He said this because there are two types of knowledge. The first produces its fruit in the heart. It is knowledge of Allah, the Exalted – His Names, His Attributes, and His Acts – which commands fear, respect, exaltation, love, supplication and reliance on Him. This is the beneficial type of knowledge. As ibn Mas'ud said: "They will recite the Qur'an, but it will not go beyond their throats. The Qur'an is only beneficial when it reaches the heart and is firmly planted in it."

Al-Hasan said: "There are two kinds of knowledge: knowledge of the tongue, which can be a case against the son of Adam, as is mentioned in the *hadith* of the Prophet ﷺ: 'The Qur'an is either a case for you or a case against you'[8]; and knowledge of the heart, which is beneficial knowledge. The second kind is the beneficial kind which raises people in rank; it is the inner knowledge which is absorbed by the heart and puts it right. The knowledge that is on the tongue is taken lightly by people: neither those who possess it, nor anyone else, act upon it, and then it vanishes when its owners vanish on the Day of Judgement, when creation will be brought to account."

Notes

1. Al-Bukhari and Muslim.
2. Al-Bukhari, *Kitab al-Qadar,* 11/499.
3. This is illustrated in a *hadith* recorded by *Imam* Muslim in his *Sahih*, in which it is related on the authority of Abu

Dharr that the Prophet Muhammad, may Allah bless him and grant him peace, said, "You will receive the reward for *sadaqa* even when you have sexual intercourse with your wives." The *sahaba* said, "Will we really be rewarded for satisfying our physical desires?" He replied, "If you have *haram* intercourse, you will be committing a sin; similarly, if you have *halal* intercourse, you will be rewarded."*Imam* an-Nawawi said, "This *hadith* clearly shows that permissible actions become acts of obedience if there is a good intention behind them; sexual intercourse becomes an act of worship if it is accompanied by any one of the following good intentions: keeping company with your wife in kindness, as Allah ta'Ala has commanded; hoping to have, as a result of the intercourse, good and righteous offspring; guarding your chastity and that of your wife; helping to prevent *haram* lustful glances or thoughts, or *haram* intercourse; and any other good intention."

4. *Tahdhib al-'Asma' li-Nawawi*, 1/173. Abu Ishaq ash-Shirazi once entered the mosque to have something to eat, as was his custom, and then realised that he had dropped a *dinar*. He retraced his steps and found it lying on the ground, but then left it where it was, saying, "Perhaps it is not mine; perhaps it belongs to somebody else."

5. *Sahih, Ja'mi 'l-'Ulum wa'l-Hikam*, p.19.

6. Al-Bukhari and Muslim.

7. Muslim, 21/17.

8. Muslim, *Kitab at-Tahara*, 3/99.

THREE

TYPES OF HEART

Just as the heart may be described in terms of being alive or dead, it may also be regarded as belonging to one of three types; these are the healthy heart, the dead heart, and the sick heart.

The Healthy Heart

On the Day of Resurrection, only those who come to Allah with a healthy heart will be saved. Allah says:

❴ The day on which neither wealth nor sons will be of any use, except for whoever brings to Allah a sound heart. (26:88-89) ❵

In defining the healthy heart, the following has been said: " It is a heart cleansed from any passion that challenges what Allah commands, or disputes what He forbids. It is free from any impulses which contradict His good. As a result, it is safeguarded against the worship of anything other than Him, and seeks the judgement of no other except that of His Messenger ﷺ. Its services are exclusively reserved for Allah, willingly and lovingly, with total reliance, relating all matters to Him, in fear, hope and sincere dedication. When it loves, its love is in the way of Allah. If it detests, it detests in the light of what He detests. When it gives, it gives for Allah. If it withholds, it withholds for Allah. Nevertheless, all this will not suffice for its salvation until it is free from following, or taking as its guide, anyone other than His Messenger ﷺ."

A servant with a healthy heart must dedicate it to its journey's end and not base his actions and speech on those of any other person except Allah's Messenger ﷺ. He must not give precedence to any other faith or words or deeds over those of Allah and His Messenger, may Allah bless him and grant him peace. Allah says:

❨ Oh you who believe, do not put yourselves above Allah and His Messenger, but fear Allah, for Allah is Hearing, Knowing. (49:1) ❩

The Dead Heart

This is the opposite of the healthy heart. It does not know its Lord and does not worship Him as He commands, in the way which He likes, and with which He is pleased. It clings instead to its lusts and desires, even if these are likely to incur Allah's displeasure and wrath. It worships things other than Allah, and its loves and its hatreds, and its giving and its withholding, arise from its whims, which are of paramount importance to it and preferred above the pleasure of Allah. Its whims are its *imam*. Its lust is its guide. Its ignorance is its leader. Its crude impulses are its impetus. It is immersed in its concern with worldly objectives. It is drunk with its own fancies and its love for hasty, fleeting pleasures. It is called to Allah and the *akhira* from a distance but it does not respond to advice, and instead it follows any scheming, cunning *shaytan*. Life angers and pleases it, and passion makes it deaf and blind[1] to anything except what is evil.

To associate and keep company with the owner of such a heart is to tempt illness: living with him is like taking poison, and befriending him means utter destruction.

The Sick Heart

This is a heart with life in it, as well as illness. The former sustains it at one moment, the latter at another, and it follows whichever one of the two manages to dominate it. It has love for Allah, faith in Him, sincerity towards Him, and reliance upon Him, and these are what give it life. It also has a craving for lust and pleasure, and prefers them, and strives to experience them. It is full of self-admiration, which can lead to its own destruction. It listens to two callers: one calling it to Allah and His Prophet ﷺ and the *akhira*; and the other calling it to the fleeting pleasures of this world. It responds to whichever one of the two happens to have most influence over it at the time.

The first heart is alive, submitted to Allah, humble, sensitive and aware; the second is brittle and dead; the third wavers between either its safety or its ruin.

Notes

1. It has been related on the authority of Abu'd-Darda' that the Messenger of Allah, may Allah bless him and grant him peace, said, "Your love for something makes you blind and deaf." Abu Daw'ud, *al-Adab*, 14/38; Ahmad, *al-Musnad*, 5/194. The *hadith* is classified as *hasan*.

FOUR

SYMPTOMS OF THE HEART'S SICKNESS AND SIGNS OF ITS HEALTH

The Signs of a Sick Heart

A servant's heart may be ill, and seriously deteriorating, while he remains oblivious of its condition. It may even die without him realising it. The symptoms of its sickness, or the signs of its death, are that its owner is not aware of the harm that results from the damage caused by wrong actions, and is unperturbed by his ignorance of the truth or by his false beliefs.

Since the living heart experiences pain as a result of any ugliness that it encounters and through its recognising its ignorance of the truth (to a degree that corresponds to its level of awareness), it is capable of recognising the onset of decay – and the increase in the severity of the remedy that will be needed to stop it – but then sometimes it prefers to put up with the pain rather than undergo the arduous trial of the cure!

Some of the many signs of the heart's sickness is its turning away from good foods to harmful ones, from good remedies to shameful sickness. The healthy heart prefers what is beneficial and healing to what is harmful and damaging; the sick heart prefers the opposite. The most beneficial sustenance for the heart is faith and the best medicine is the Qur'an.

The Signs of a Healthy Heart

For the heart to be healthy it should depart from this life and arrive in the next, and then settle there as if it were one of its people; it only came to this life as a passer-by, taking whatever provisions it needed and then returning home. As the Prophet, may Allah bless him and grant him peace, said to Abdullah ibn Umar, "Be in this world as if you were a stranger or a passer-by."[1] The more diseased the heart is, the more it desires this world; it dwells in it until it becomes like one of its own people.

This healthy heart continues to trouble its owner until he returns to Allah, and is at peace with Him, and joins Him, like a lover driven by compulsion who finally reaches his beloved. Besides his love for Him he needs no other, and after invoking Him no other invocations are needed. Serving Him precludes the need to serve any other.

If this heart misses its share of reciting the Qur'an and invoking Allah, or completing one of the prescribed acts of worship, then its owner suffers more distress than a cautious man who suffers because of the loss of money or a missed opportunity to make it. It longs to serve, just as a famished person longs for food and drink.

Yahya ibn Mu'adh said: "Whoever is pleased with serving Allah, everything will be pleased to serve him; and whoever finds pleasure in contemplating Allah, all the people will find pleasure in contemplating him."

This heart has only one concern: that all its actions, and its inner thoughts and utterances, are obedient to Allah. It is more careful with its time than the meanest people are with their money, so that it will not be spent wastefully. When it enters into the prayer, all its worldly worries and anxieties vanish and it finds its comfort and bliss in adoring its Lord. It does not cease to mention Allah, nor tire of serving Him, and it finds intimate company with no-one save a person who guides it to Allah and reminds it of Him.

Its attention to the correctness of its action is greater than its attention to the action itself. It is scrupulous in making sure that the intentions behind its actions are sincere and pure and that they result in good deeds.

As well as and in spite of all this, it not only testifies to the generosity of Allah in giving it the opportunity to carry out such actions, but also testifies to its own imperfection and shortcomings in executing them.

The Causes of Sickness of the Heart

The temptations to which the heart is exposed are what cause its sickness. These are the temptations of desires and fancies. The former cause intentions and the will to be corrupted, and the latter cause knowledge and belief to falter.

Hudhayfa ibn al-Yamani, may Allah be pleased with him, said: "The Messenger of Allah ﷺ said, 'Temptations are presented to the heart, one by one. Any heart that accepts them will be left with a black stain, but any heart that rejects them will be left with a mark of purity, so that hearts are of two types: a dark heart that has turned away and become like an overturned vessel, and a pure heart that will never be harmed by temptation for as long as the earth and the heavens exist. The dark heart only recognises good and denounces evil when this suits its desires and whims.'" [2]

He, may Allah bless him and grant him peace, placed hearts, when exposed to temptation, into two categories:

First, a heart which, when it is exposed to temptation, absorbs it like a sponge that soaks up water, leaving a black stain in it. It continues to absorb each temptation that is offered to it until it is darkened and corrupted, which is what he meant by "like an overturned vessel". When this happens, two dangerous sicknesses take hold of it and plunge it into ruin:

The first is that of its confusing good with evil, to such an extent that it does not recognise the former and does not denounce the latter. This sickness may even gain hold of it to such an extent that it believes good to be evil and vice-versa, the *sunnah* to be *bida'* and vice-versa, the truth to be false and falsity to be the truth.

The second is that of its setting up its desires as its judge, over and above what the Prophet ﷺ taught, so that it is enslaved and led by its whims and fancies.

Second, a pure heart in which the light of faith is bright and from which its radiance shines. When temptation is presented to pure hearts such as this, they oppose it and reject it, and so their light and illumination only increase.

Notes

1. Al-Bukhari, *Kitab ar-Riqaq*, 11/233.
2. Muslim, *Kitab al-Iman*, 2/170 (with different wording).

FIVE

THE FOUR POISONS OF THE HEART

You should know that all acts of disobedience are poison to the heart and cause its sickness and ruin. They result in its will running off course, against that of Allah, and so its sickness festers and increases. Ibn al-Mubarak said:

> I have seen wrong actions killing hearts,
> And their degradation may lead to
> their becoming addicted to them.
> Turning away from wrong actions
> gives life to the hearts,
> And opposing your self is best for it.

Whoever is concerned with the health and life of his heart, must rid it of the effects of such poisons, and then protect it by avoiding new ones. If he takes any by mistake, then he should hasten to wipe out their effect by turning in repentance and seeking forgiveness from Allah, as well as by doing good deeds that will wipe out his wrong actions.

By the four poisons we mean unnecessary talking, unrestrained glances, too much food and keeping bad company. Of all the poisons, these are the most widespread and have the greatest effect on a heart's well-being.

Unnecessary Talking

It is reported in *al-Musnad*, on the authority of Anas, that the Prophet ﷺ said: "The faith of a servant is not put right until his heart is put right, and his heart is not put right until his tongue is put right."¹ This shows that the Prophet ﷺ has made the purification of faith conditional on the purification of the heart, and the purification of the heart conditional on the purification of the tongue.

At-Tirmidhi relates in a *hadith* on the authority of Ibn Umar: "Do not talk excessively without remembering Allah, because such excessive talk without the mention of Allah causes the heart to harden, and the person furthest from Allah is a person with a hard heart."²

Umar Ibn al-Khattab, may Allah be pleased with him, said: "A person who talks too much is a person who often makes mistakes, and someone who often makes mistakes, often has wrong actions. The Fire has a priority over such a frequent sinner."³

In a *hadith* related on the authority of Mu'adh, the Prophet ﷺ said, "Shall I not tell you how to control all that?" I said, "Yes do, O Messenger of Allah." So he held his tongue between his fingers, and then he said: "Restrain this." I said, "O Prophet of Allah, are we accountable for what we say?" He ﷺ said, "May your mother be bereft by your loss! Is there anything more than the harvest of the tongues that throws people on their faces (or he said 'on their noses') into the Fire?"⁴

What is meant here by 'the harvest of the tongues' is the punishment for saying forbidden things. A man, through his actions and words, sows the seeds of either good or evil. On the Day of Resurrection he harvests their fruits. Those who sow the seeds of good words and deeds harvest honour and blessings; those who sow the seeds of evil words and deeds reap only regret and remorse.

A *hadith* related by Abu Huraira says, "What mostly causes people to be sent to the Fire are the two openings:

the mouth and the private parts." [5]

Abu Huraira also related that the Messenger of Allah ﷺ said, "The servant speaks words, the consequences of which he does not realise, and for which he is sent down into the depths of the Fire further than the distance between the east and the west." [6]

The same *hadith* was transmitted by at-Tirmidhi with slight variations: "The servant says something that he thinks is harmless, and for which he will be plunged into the depths of the Fire as far as seventy autumns." [7]

Uqba ibn Amir said: "I said: 'O Messenger of Allah, what is our best way of surviving?' He, may Allah bless him and grant him peace, replied: 'Guard your tongue, make your house suffice for sheltering your privacy, and weep for your wrong actions.'" [8]

It has been related on the authority of Sahl ibn Sa'd that the Prophet ﷺ said, "Whoever can guarantee what is between his jaws and what is between his legs, I guarantee him the Garden." [9]

It has also been related by Abu Huraira, may Allah be pleased with him, that the Prophet, may Allah bless him and grant him peace, said, "Let whoever believes in Allah and the Last Day either speak good or remain silent." [10]

Thus talking can either be good, in which case it is commendable, or bad, in which case it is *haram*.

The Prophet ﷺ said: "Everything the children of Adam say goes against them, except for their enjoining good and forbidding evil, and remembering Allah, Glorious and Mighty is He." This was reported by at-Tirmidhi and Ibn Ma'jah on the authority of Umm Habiba, may Allah be pleased with her. [11]

Umar ibn al-Khattab visited Abu Bakr, may Allah be pleased with them, and found him pulling his tongue with his fingers. Umar said "Stop! may Allah forgive you!" Abu Bakr replied: "This tongue has brought me to dangerous places." [12]

Abdullah ibn Mas'ud said: "By Allah, besides Whom no god exists, nothing deserves a long prison sentence more than my tongue." He also used to say: "O tongue, say good and you will profit; desist from saying evil things and you will be safe; otherwise you will find only regret."

Abu Huraira reported that Ibn al-Abbas said: "A person will not feel greater fury or anger for any part of his body on the Day of Judgement more than what he will feel for his tongue, unless he only used it for saying or enjoining good."

Al-Hassan said: "Whoever does not hold his tongue cannot understand his *deen*."

The least harmful of a tongue's faults is talking about whatever does not concern it. The following *hadith* of the Prophet ﷺ is enough to indicate the harm of this fault: "One of the merits of a person's Islam is his abandoning what does not concern him." [13]

Abu Ubaida related that al-Hassan said: "One of the signs of Allah's abandoning a servant is His making him preoccupied with what does not concern him."

Sahl said, "Whoever talks about what does not concern him is deprived of truthfulness."

As we have already mentioned above, this is the least harmful of the tongue's faults. There are far worse things, like backbiting, gossiping, obscene and misleading talk, two-faced and hypocritical talk, showing off, quarrelling, bickering, singing, lying, mockery, derision and falsehood; and there are many more faults which can affect a servant's tongue, ruining his heart and causing him to lose both his happiness and pleasure in this life, and his success and profit in the next life. Allah is the One to Whom we turn for assistance.

Unrestrained Glances

The unrestrained glance results in the one who looks becoming attracted to what he sees, and in the imprinting of an image of what he sees in his heart. This can result in several kinds of corruption in the heart of the servant. The following are a number of them:

It has been related that the Prophet 鬱 once said words to the effect: "The glance is a poisoned arrow of *shaytan*. Whoever lowers his gaze for Allah, He will bestow upon him a refreshing sweetness which he will find in his heart on the day that he meets Him." [14]

Shaytan enters with the glance, for he travels with it, faster than the wind blowing through an empty place. He makes what is seen appear more beautiful than it really is, and transforms it into an idol for the heart to worship. Then he promises it false rewards, lights the fire of desires within it, and fuels it with the wood of forbidden actions, which the servant would not have committed had it not been for this distorted image.

This distracts the heart and makes it forget its more important concerns. It stands between it and them; and so the heart loses its straight path and falls into the pit of desire and ignorance. Allah, Mighty and Glorious is He, says:

❨ And do not obey anyone whose heart We have made forgetful in remembering Us – who follows his own desires, and whose affair has exceeded all bounds. (18:28)❩

The unrestrained gaze causes all three afflictions.

It has been said that between the eye and the heart is an immediate connection; if the eyes are corrupted, then the heart follows. It becomes like a rubbish heap where all the dirt and filth and rottenness collect, and so there is no room for love for Allah, relating all matters to Him, awareness of being in His presence, and feeling joy at His proximity – only the opposite of these things can inhabit such a heart.

Staring and gazing without restraint is disobedience to Allah:

❴ Tell the believing men to lower their gaze and guard their modesty; that is more purifying for them. Surely Allah is aware of what they do. (24:30) ❵

Only the one who obeys Allah's commands is content in this world, and only the servant who obeys Allah will survive in the next world.

Furthermore, letting the gaze roam free cloaks the heart with darkness, just as lowering the gaze for Allah clothes it in light. After the above *ayah*, Allah, the Glorious and Mighty, says in the same *surah* of the Qur'an:

❴ Allah is the light of the heavens and the earth: the likeness of His light is as if there were a niche, and in the niche is a lamp, and in the lamp is a glass, and the glass as it were a brilliant star, lit from a blessed tree, an olive, neither of the east nor of the west, whose oil is well nigh luminous, though fire scarce touched it. Light upon light. Allah guides whomever He wants to His Light. Allah strikes metaphors for man; and Allah knows all things. (24:35) ❵

When the heart is a light, countless good comes to it from all directions. If it is dark, then clouds of evil and afflictions come from all directions to cover it up.

Letting the gaze run loose also makes the heart blind to distinguishing between truth and falsehood, between the *sunnah* and innovation; while lowering it for Allah, the Mighty and Exalted, gives it a penetrating, true and distinguishing insight.

A righteous man once said: "Whoever enriches his outward behaviour by following the *sunnah* , and makes his inward soul wealthy through contemplation, and averts his gaze away from looking at what is forbidden, and avoids anything of a doubtful nature, and feeds solely on what is *halal* – his inner sight will never falter."

Rewards for actions come in kind. Whoever lowers his gaze from what Allah has forbidden, Allah will give his inner sight abundant light.

Too Much Food

The consumption of small amounts of food guarantees tenderness of the heart, strength of the intellect, humility of the self, weakness of desires, and gentleness of temperament. Immoderate eating brings about the opposite of these praiseworthy qualities.

Al-Miqdam ibn Ma'd Yakrib said: "I heard the Messenger of Allah ﷺ say: 'The son of Adam fills no vessel more displeasing to Allah than his stomach. A few morsels should be enough for him to preserve his strength. If he must fill it, then he should allow a third for his food, a third for his drink and leave a third empty for easy breathing.'" [15]

Excessive eating induces many kinds of harm. It makes the body incline towards disobedience to Allah and makes worship and obedience seem laborious – such evils are bad enough in themselves. A full stomach and excessive eating have caused many a wrong action and inhibited much worship. Whoever safeguards against the evils of overfilling his stomach has prevented great evil. It is easier for *shaytan* to control a person who has filled his stomach with food and drink, which is why it has often been said: "Restrict the pathways of *shaytan* by fasting." [16]

It has been reported that when a group of young men from the Tribe of Israel were worshipping, and it was time for them to break their fast, a man stood up and said: "Do not eat too much, otherwise you will drink too much, and then you will end up sleeping too much, and then you will lose too much."

The Prophet 變 and his companions, may Allah be pleased with them, used to go hungry quite frequently. Although this was often due to a shortage of food, Allah decreed the best and most favourable conditions for His Messenger, may Allah bless him and grant him peace. This is why Ibn Umar and his father before him – in spite of the abundance of food available to them – modelled their eating habits on those of the Prophet 變. It has been reported that Aisha, may Allah be pleased with her, said: "From the time of their arrival in Madina up until his death 變, the family of Muhammed 變 never ate their fill of bread made from wheat three nights in a row." [17]

Ibrahim ibn Adham said: "Any one who controls his stomach is in control of his *deen*, and anyone who controls his hunger is in control of good behaviour. Disobedience towards Allah is nearest to a person who is satiated with a full stomach, and furthest away from a person who is hungry."

Keeping Bad Company

Unnecessary companionship is a chronic disease that causes much harm. How often have the wrong kind of companionship and intermixing deprived people of Allah's generosity, planting discord in their hearts which even the passage of time – even if it were long enough for mountains to be worn away – has been unable to dispel. In keeping such company one can find the roots of loss, both in this life and in the next life.

A servant should benefit from companionship. In order to do so he should divide people into four categories, and be careful not to get them mixed up, for once one of them is mixed with another, then evil can find its way through to him:

The **first** category are those people whose company is like food: it is indispensable, night or day. Once a servant has taken his need from it, he leaves it be until he requires it again, and so on. These are the people with knowledge of Allah – of His commands, of the scheming of His enemies, and of the diseases of the heart and their remedies – who wish well for Allah, His Prophet 鐕 and His servants. Associating with this type of person is an achievement in itself.

The **second** category are those people whose company is like a medicine. They are only required when a disease sets in. When you are healthy, you have no need of them. However, mixing with them is sometimes necessary for your livelihood, businesses, consultation and the like. Once what you need from them has been fulfilled, mixing with them should be avoided.

The **third** category are those people whose company is harmful. Mixing with this type of person is like a disease, in all its variety and degrees and strengths and weaknesses. Associating with one or some of them is like an incurable chronic disease. You will never profit either in this life or in the next life if you have them for company, and you will surely lose either one or both of your *deen* and your livelihood because of them. If their companionship has taken hold of you and is established, then it becomes a fatal, terrifying sickness.

Amongst such people are those who neither speak any good that might benefit you, nor listen closely to you so that they might benefit from you. They do not know their souls and consequently put their selves in their rightful place. If they speak, their words fall on their listeners' hearts like the lashes of a cane, while all the while they are full of admiration for and delight in their own words.

They cause distress to those in their company, while believing that they are the sweet scent of the gathering. If they are silent, they are heavier than a massive millstone – too heavy to carry or even drag across the floor. [18]

All in all, mixing with anyone who is bad for the soul will not last, even if it is unavoidable. It can be one of the most distressing aspects of a servant's life that he is plagued by such person, with whom it may be necessary to associate. In such a relationship, a servant should cling to good behaviour, only presenting him with his outward appearance, while disguising his inner soul, until Allah offers him a way out of his affliction and the means of escape from this situation.

The **fourth** category are those people whose company is doom itself. It is like taking poison: its victim either finds an antidote or perishes. Many people belong to this category. They are the people of religious innovation and misguidance, those who abandon the *sunnah* of the Messenger of Allah ﷺ and advocate other beliefs. They call what is the *sunnah* a *bid'a* and vice-versa. A man with any intellect should not sit in their assemblies nor mix with them. The result of doing so will either be the death of his heart or, at the very best, its falling seriously ill.

What Gives the Heart Life and Sustenance

You should know that acts of obedience are essential to the well being of the servant's heart, just in the same way that food and drink are to that of the body. All wrong actions are the same as poisonous foods, and they inevitably harm the heart.

The servant feels the need to worship his Lord, Mighty and Glorious is He, for he is naturally in constant need of His help and assistance.

In order to maintain the well being of his body, the servant carefully follows a strict diet. He habitually and constantly eats good food at regular intervals, and is quick to free his stomach of harmful elements if he happens to eat bad food by mistake.

The well being of the servant's heart, however, is far more important than that of his body, for while the well being of his body enables him to lead a life that is free from illnesses in this world, that of the heart ensures him both a fortunate life in this world and eternal bliss in the next.

In the same way, while the death of the body cuts the servant off from this world, the death of the heart results in everlasting anguish. A righteous man once said, "How odd, that some people mourn for the one whose body has died, but never mourn for the one whose heart has died – and yet the death of the heart is far more serious!"

Thus acts of obedience are indispensable to the well being of the heart. It is worthwhile mentioning the following acts of obedience here, since they are very necessary and essential for the servant's heart:

Dhikr of Allah ta'Ala, recitation of the Noble Qur'an, seeking Allah's forgiveness, making *du'as*, invoking Allah's blessings and peace on the Prophet, may Allah bless him and grant him peace, and praying at night.

Notes

1. *Da'if hadith*, Al-Mundhari, 3/234; and al-Iraqi in *al-Ihya*, 8/1539.
2. *Da'if hadith*, at-Tirmidhi, *Kitab az-Zuhud*, 7/92,*gharib*; no one else has transmitted it other than Ibrahim ibn Abdullah ibn Hatib, whom ath-Thahabi mentions, 1/43, stating that this is one of the *gharib hadith* attributed to him.
3. *Da'if hadith*, Ibn Hibban and al-Baihaqi, and al-Iraqi in his edition of *al-Ihya*, 8/1541.
4. *Sahih hadith*, at-Tirmidhi, al-Hakim, ath-Thahabi.
5. *Sahih hadith*, at-Tirmidhi and Ahmad; also al-Hakim and ath-Thahabi.
6. Al-Bukhari in *Kitab ar-Riqaq*, and Muslim in *Kitab az-Zuhud*.
7. At-Tirmidhi, *Kitab az-Zuhud*; he said the *hadith* is *hasan gharib*.
8. At-Tirmidhi in *Kitab az-Zuhud* with a slightly different wording; he said the *hadith* is *hasan*. This wording is reported by Abu Na'im in *al-Hilya*.
9. Al-Bukhari, *Kitab ar-Riqaq*, 11/308 and *Kitab al-Hudud*, 12/113.
10. Al-Bukhari, *Kitab ar-Riqaq*, 11/308; Muslim, *Kitab al-Iman*, 2/18. The complete *hadith* is: "Let whoever believes in Allah and the Last Day either speak good or remain silent; and let whoever believes in Allah and the Last Day be generous to his neighbour; and let whoever believes in Allah and the Last Day be generous to his guest. "

11. The *hadith* is *hasan* and is reported by at-Tirmidhi in *Kitab az-Zuhud* and by Ibn Majah in *Kitab al-Fitan*. At-Tirmidhi classifies it as *hasan gharib*. We have no report of it other than from Muhammad ibn Yazid ibn Khanis.

12. *Hasan* according to Abu Ya'la, Baihaqi and as-Suyuti.

13. *Sahih*, at-Tirmidhi, *Kitab az-Zuhud*, 6/607; Ahmad, *al-Musnad*, 1/201; as-Sa'ati, *al-Fath ar-Rabbani*, 19/257; *hadith* number 12 in an-Nawawi's *Forty Hadiths*.

14. *Da'if*, at-Tabarani, 8/63; al-Hakim, *al-Mustadrak*, 4/314; Ahmad, *al-Musnad*, 5/264.

15. *Sahih*, Ahmad, *al-Musnad*, 4/132; as-Sa'ati, *al-Fath ar-Rabbani*, 17/88; at-Tirmidhi, *Kitab az-Zuhud*, 7/51.

16. *Da'if*; it does not appear in most of the sources of the *sunnah*, but is mentioned in al-Ghazzali's *al-Ihya*, 8/1488.

17. Al-Bukhari, *Kitab al-At'ima*, 9/549; and Muslim, *Kitab az-Zuhud*, 8/105.

18. Ash-Shafi', may Allah be pleased with him, is reported to have said, "Whenever a tedious person sits next to me, the side on which he is sitting feels lower down than the other side to me."

SIX

REMEMBRANCE OF ALLAH
AND RECITATION OF THE QUR'AN

Ibn Taimiyya wrote, "Remembrance of Allah is to the heart what water is to fish. What happens to a fish when it is taken out of water?" *Imam* Shams ad-Din ibn al-Qayyim wrote about nearly eighty benefits that come with *dhikru'llah* in his book *al-Wabil al-Sayyib*. We shall quote some of them here, although we recommend the reader to refer to this book itself because of its great value.

Remembrance of Allah is sustenance for both the heart and the spirit. If the servant is deprived of it he becomes like a body which has been deprived of food.

Remembrance of Allah also drives away *shaytan*, suppressing him and breaking him; it is pleasing to the Merciful, Mighty and Exalted is He, dispels worry and melancholy from the heart, adorns it with delight and joy, fills the heart and face with light, and cloaks the one who remembers Allah with dignity, gentleness and freshness. It instils love for Allah, fear of Him, and relating all matters to Him. It also enhances Allah's remembrance of His servant, for as Allah says:

❲ So remember Me – I will remember you. (2:152) ❳

Even if this were the only reward for the remembrance of Allah, it would be mercy and honour enough, for such a heart is always aware and free from wrong actions.

Although remembrance is one of the easiest forms of worship, the mercy and honour that it brings cannot be achieved by any other means. Abu Huraira reported that the Prophet ﷺ said, "Whoever recites the words, 'There is no god but Allah, the One, having no partner with Him. Sovereignty belongs to Him and All praise is due to Him, and He is Powerful over everything', one hundred times every day, there is a reward equal to freeing ten slaves for him, and a hundred good actions are recorded for him, and a hundred wrong actions are removed from his record. That is a safeguard for him against *shaytan* on that day until evening, and no one brings anything more excellent than this, except the one who has done more than this (that is, who recites these words more than one hundred times)." [1]

Jabir reported that the Prophet ﷺ said, "Whoever recites the words, 'Glory be to Allah and His is the praise', will have a palm tree planted for him in the Garden." [2]

Ibn Mas'ud, may Allah be pleased with him, said, "To Praise Allah, may He be Exalted, is more dear to me than spending the same number of *dinars* (as the number of times I praise Him) in the way of Allah."

Remembrance of Allah is a remedy for hard hearts. A man once told al-Hassan, "O Abu Sa'id, I complain to you about the hardness of my heart." He said, "Soften it with the remembrance of Allah." Makhul said, "Remembrance of Allah is (a sign of) health, while remembrance of people is like a disease." A man once asked Salman, "Which deeds are the best?" He said, "Haven't you read in the Qur'an:

❨And the remembrance of Allah is greatest. (29:45) ❩?"

Abu Musa once related that the Prophet 變 said, "The difference between the one who remembers his Lord and the one who does not is like the difference between the living and the dead." [3]

Abdullah ibn Busr related that a man once told the Prophet 變 , "The roads to good are many and I am unable to take all of them, so please tell me something to which I can hold fast, but do not overburden me lest I forget it." He said, "Make sure that your tongue is moist and supple with the remembrance of Allah, the Exalted." [4]

Continual remembrance of Allah increases a servant's good witnesses on the Day of Resurrection. It is a means which prevents him from talking in the wrong way, such as backbiting and spreading tales and their like. Either the tongue is mentioning Allah and remembering Him, or it is talking incorrectly.

Whoever has the gates of remembrance opened to him has an opening to his Lord, Mighty and Glorious is He, through which he will find what he seeks. If he finds Allah, he has found everything. If he misses the opportunity, he has missed everything.

There are several types of remembrance. The remembrance of the Names of Allah, Mighty and Glorious is He, the remembrance of His Attributes, and praising Him and thanking Him. All of these can take the form of saying, for example , 'Glory be to Allah', 'Praise be to Allah', 'There is no god but Allah'. A servant can also remember Allah by referring to His Names and Attributes, such as by saying, for example, "Allah, Mighty and Glorious is He, Hears all that his servants say and do"; or by mentioning what He has commanded and what He has forbidden, such as saying, "Allah, the Mighty and Glorious, commands such and such, or forbids such and such".

A servant can also remember Allah by talking about His blessings, while the best type of remembrance is the recitation of the Qur'an, because this contains remedies to cure the heart from all illnesses. Allah, the Exalted, says:

❴ O mankind, there has come to you a protection from your Lord and a healing for what is in your hearts, and for those who believe, a guidance and a mercy. (10:57)❵

And also:

❴ We send down in the Qur'an that which is a healing and a mercy for those who believe. (17:82) ❵

All the illnesses of the heart result from desires and doubt, and the Qur'an is a cure for both. It has enough clear signs and proofs to distinguish between truth and falsehood, and thus it cures the diseases of doubt which ruin knowledge, understanding and perception, by enabling a person to see things as they really are.

Whoever studies the Qur'an, and allows it to be absorbed by his heart, will recognise truth and falsehood and will be able to distinguish between them, just as he is able to distinguish between night and day.

As for curing the diseases that arise from desires, it is because it contains wisdom and good counsel. This recommends avoiding worldly gains and inspires a yearning for the *akhira*.

The Prophet ﷺ once said, "Whoever wants to love Allah and His Messenger should read the Qur'an." [5]

The Qur'an is also the best means for bringing the servant nearer to his Lord, Glorious and Exalted is He. Khabbab ibn al-Arat said to a man, "Draw closer to Allah as much as you can, and remember that you can do so by no means more pleasing to Him than using His own words."

Ibn Mas'ud said, "Whoever loves the Qur'an loves Allah and His Messenger," and *sayyedina* Uthman ibn Affan, may Allah be pleased with him, said, "If your hearts were really pure, they would never have enough of reciting Allah's words."

All in all, the most beneficial thing for the servant is to remember Allah, Mighty and Glorious is He, constantly:

❴ Surely in the remembrance of Allah do hearts find rest. (13:28) ❵

The best kind of remembrance is to recite the Book of Allah, the Glorious and Exalted.

Notes

1. Al-Bukhari, *Kitab ad-Da'awat*, 11/201; Muslim, *Kitab adh-Dhikr wa'd-Du'a*, 17/16.
2. *Sahih*, at-Tirmidhi, *Kitab ad-Da'awat*, 9/433.
3. Al-Bukhari, *Kitab ad-Da'awat*, 11/208; al-Hakim, *Kitab ad-Du'a*, 1/495.
4. At-Tirmidhi, *Kitab ad-Da'awat*, 9/314.
5. *Da'if, munkar*. See the commentary on this *hadith* in Ibn Hajar's *Tahdhib at-Tahdhib*, 2/222 and *Lisan al-Mizan*, 2/185, and in as-Suyuti's *Al-Jami' as-Saghir*, 6/150.

SEVEN

SEEKING ALLAH'S FORGIVENESS

Forgiveness is being shielded from the harmful consequences of wrong actions, and the veiling of them. Seeking
forgiveness is mentioned again and again in the Qur'an,
and in some places it is a command, as in His saying,
Glorious and Exalted is He:

❰ And seek forgiveness of Allah; surely Allah is Forgiving, Compassionate. (73:20) ❱

In other places, Allah praises those who seek His forgiveness, as in the *ayah*:

❰ And those who pray for forgiveness in the early
hours of the morning. (3:17) ❱

In other places, Allah tells us that He forgives those who
ask for His forgiveness, as in the *ayah*:

❰ And whoever does evil, or wrongs his own soul, but
afterwards seeks Allah's forgiveness, will find Allah is
Forgiving, Compassionate. (4:110) ❱

Seeking forgiveness is frequently associated with repentance, in which case it takes the form of asking for forgiveness with the tongue. Repentance is turning away
from wrong actions with both heart and body. Seeking forgiveness is similar to supplication in that Allah, if He so
wishes, responds to it and forgives the person who seeks
His forgiveness. This is especially true if the *du'a* came di-

rectly from a heart troubled by wrong actions, or if it was made during the times most favourable for His response, such as in the early hours of the morning or immediately following the prayer.

It has been transmitted that Luqman once told his son, "O my son, make it a habit for your tongue to utter the words, 'Forgive me, O Allah', for there are certain times during which Allah will not disappoint a servant who calls on Him."

Al-Hasan said, "Ask for Allah's forgiveness frequently – in your homes, at your tables, on your roads, in your markets, at your meetings, wherever you are. You never know when you will be granted His forgiveness."

Abu Huraira reported that the Prophet ﷺ said, "I swear by Allah that I supplicate for Allah's forgiveness and turn to Him in repentance more than seventy times a day." [1]

Abu Huraira said, "I heard the Messenger of Allah ﷺ say, 'A servant committed a sin and he said, "O Allah, I have committed a sin, so forgive me." Allah said, "Does My servant know that he has a Lord Who forgives sins and helps him? I forgive My servant." After some time, the man committed another sin so he said, "O my Lord, I have committed another sin, so forgive me." His Lord said, "Does My servant know that he has a Lord Who forgives sins and helps him? I forgive My servant." After some time, the man committed yet another sin so he said, "O my Lord, I have committed another sin, so forgive me." His Lord said, "Does My servant know that he has a Lord Who forgives sins and helps him? O servant, do what you like. I have granted you forgiveness."'" [2]

He, Exalted is He, said this three times.

This means that the man was granted forgiveness because he continued to seek Allah's forgiveness each time he committed a sin. It appears that this applied so long as his seeking forgiveness was not accompanied by the intention to repeat the sin again afterwards.

Aisha, may Allah be pleased with her, said, "It is a fortunate person who (on the Day of Judgement) finds in his record many *du'as* for forgiveness."

In other words, seeking Allah's forgiveness is a cure for all wrong actions.

Qatada said, "This Qur'an guides you to the recognition of your illnesses and to their remedies. Your illnesses are your sins and your medicine is seeking Allah's forgiveness."

Ali ibn Abi Talib, may Allah be pleased with him, said, "Allah does not inspire seeking forgiveness in any servant whom He wishes to punish."

Notes

1. Al-Bukhari, *Kitab ad-Da'awat*, 11/101.
2. Al-Bukhari, *Kitab at-Tawhid*, 13/466; Muslim, *Kitab adh-Dhikr wa'd-Du'a*, 17/75.

EIGHT

SUPPLICATION

Allah, Mighty and Glorious is He, has commanded us to supplicate to Him and has promised to respond to us when we do so. He says:

❨ Call on Me – I will answer you. (40:60) ❩

Then He follows this by saying:

❨ Surely those who are too arrogant to worship Me will enter Hell in humiliation. (40:60) ❩

Praise be to Allah, the Most Mighty, Who has boundless generosity and endless mercy. He has made the servant's supplication for the fulfillment of his needs and the accomplishment of his endeavours a rewardable act of worship, which He has asked of him and which He has severely reprimanded when he neglects it, by describing him as being arrogant.

Abu Huraira has related that the Prophet ﷺ said, "Whoever does not supplicate to Allah invokes His wrath." [1]

He is so right who said:

Do not ask the son of Adam to fulfil a need,
Ask Him Whose gates are never concealed.
Allah is wrathful when you do not ask Him,
While the son of Adam is angered if you ask him.

Allah, the Mighty and Glorious, says:

❴ Is not He (best) Who answers the one who has been wronged when he calls on Him, and removes the evil? (27:62) ❵

And also:

❴ And when My servants ask you about Me, I am indeed near (to them); I answer the prayer of every supplicant when he calls on Me. (2:186) ❵

An-Nu'man ibn Bashir said, "The Messenger of Allah ﷺ said, 'Supplication is worship itself.' Then he recited the *ayah*:

❴ And your Lord has said, 'Call on Me – I will answer you'. Surely those who are too arrogant to worship Me will enter Hell in humiliation. (40:60) ❵" [2]

According to the above *ayat*, any supplication that fulfils the correct requirements will, most surely, be answered by Allah. This is further confirmed by the following *ahadith*:

"Allah is the Ever-Living, the Most Generous, and if a man raises his hands in supplication, He will be ashamed to let them be lowered disappointed and empty." [3]

Anas related that the Prophet ﷺ said, "Do not give up supplicating, for no one who supplicates is ruined." [4]

Abu Sa'id al-Khudri related that the Prophet ﷺ said, "No Muslim makes a *du'a* to Allah, without being granted one of three things by Allah: it hastens the fulfilment of what he has asked for; or it is saved up for him until the Day of Judgement; or it prevents a similar kind of trouble from happening to him – unless it was for something bad, or something that might break family ties." [5]

Umar ibn al-Khattab, may Allah be pleased with him,

said, "I do not have any anxiety about the answer, but I worry about the *du'a* itself, because anyone who is inspired by Allah to make *du'as* immediately invokes His response when he makes the *du'a*."

Good Observances in Making Supplication

These include choosing the special times for supplicating, such as on the day of *Arafat* from the days of the year, the month of Ramadan from the months of the year, Friday from among the days of the week, and the early morning hours from the times of the day.

They also include choosing favourable conditions, such as at the time of rain fall, at the time that armies fighting in the way of Allah march out, and at the time of being in the position of *sajdah*. Abu Huraira reported that the Prophet ﷺ said, "A servant is nearest to his Lord when he is in prostration, so increase your supplication when in prostration." [6]

The same applies to the time between the *adhan* and the *iqama*. The Messenger of Allah, may Allah bless him and grant him peace, said, "Supplication made during the time between the *adhan* and the *iqama* is never made in vain." [7]

It is good to be firm when supplicating and confident in Allah's response. The Prophet ﷺ said, "None of you should say, 'O Allah, forgive me if You wish' or 'O Allah, have mercy on me if You wish,' but he should always be firm in asking Allah, for nobody can compel Allah to do something against His will." [8]

It is also good to be in *wudu*, to be facing towards Makka, and to repeat the *du'a* three times. [9]

The supplication should begin with praise of Allah, by referring to His Names and His Attributes and His blessings, followed by invoking His blessings on the Messenger of Allah 灩. Then the one who asks should describe his needs and make his requests, and then finally conclude with reciting more prayers on the Prophet 灩, and praise of Allah, Mighty and Glorious is He.

It is important that his need is pure and that he does not ask for something bad or something that might cause the breaking of family ties.

The one who asks should not insist on the immediate fulfilment of his wishes, nor should he say, "I prayed to Allah, but He has not responded to my *du'a*." Abu Huraira reported that the Prophet 灩 said, "The supplication of any one of you will be fulfilled (by Allah), provided he does not become so impatient as to say, 'I asked, but my request has not been fulfilled.'" [10]

Ibn Battal said, "What is implied here is that the person despairs and accordingly gives up making *du'a* altogether – in which case it is as if it is he who has condescended to make a *du'a*, or that he considers his *du'a* sufficient to warrant a response, and so he expects an immediate response without any delay from the generous Lord – when neither does His responding to *du'as* diminish His absolute power, nor does His granting His creatures' requests decrease what He has in the least."

This *hadith* indicates one of the fine courtesies in making *du'as*, which is that the one who asks should persist and not despair of receiving a positive response to his *du'a*, for this demonstrates his submission and his absolute reliance on Allah's assistance.

Notes

1. *Hasan*, at-Tirmidhi, *Kitab ad-Da'awat*, 9/313; Ibn Ma'jah, *Kitab ad-Du'a*, 2/1258; al-Hakim, *Kitab ad-Du'a*, 1/491.

2. At-Tirmidhi, *Kitab ad-Da'awat*, 9/311; al-Hakim, *al-Mustadrak*, 1/491; an-Nawawi, *al-Adhkar*, p.525.

3. *Hasan*, at-Tirmidhi, *Kitab ad-Da'awat*, 9/544; al-Hakim, *Kitab ad-Du'a*, 1/497; Abu Da'wud, *Kitab ad-Du'a*, 1/497.

4. *Da'if*, al-Hakim, *al-Mustadrak*, 1/493; Ibn Hibban, *al-Ad'iyya*, p.596.

5. *Sahih*, at-Tirmidhi, *Kitab ad-Da'awat*, 9/923.

6. Muslim, *Kitab as-Salah*, 4/200.

7. *Sahih*, at-Tirmidhi, *Kitab as-Salah*, 1/624, and in *Kitab ad-Da'awat*, 10/53; Abu Da'wud, *Kitab as-Salah*, 2/224.

8. Al-Bukhari, *Kitab at-Tawhid*, 13/448, and in *Kitab ad-Da'awat*, 11/139; Muslim, *Kitab adh-Dhikr wa'd-Du'a*, 17/7.

9. Muslim, *Kitab al-Jihad*, 12/152. This is part of a long *hadith* related by Abu Su'ud, may Allah be pleased with him.

10. Al-Bukhari, *Kitab ad-Da'awat*, 11/140; Muslim, *Kitab adh-Dhikr wa'd-Du'a*, 17/51.

NINE

INVOKING BLESSINGS
ON THE PROPHET ﷺ

There is a *hadith* related by Abu Huraira in which it is reported that the Prophet ﷺ said, "If anyone invokes blessings on me once, Allah will grant him ten blessings." [1]

This is because one good deed is recorded as ten good
deeds, and invoking blessings on the Prophet ﷺ is one of
the most excellent things a Muslim can do.

Ibn al-Arabi said, "If someone asks about the merit of
Allah's saying ❨ Whoever does good shall be given ten
times as much. (6:160) ❩, we would say, "It has great merit.
The Qur'an has stated that a good deed is multiplied by
ten, and invoking blessings on the Messenger of Allah ﷺ
is, according to the Qur'an, a good deed which accordingly
gives the one who does it ten grades in the Garden. The
Prophet ﷺ has said that Allah blesses ten times the one
who invokes blessings on him ﷺ once. Allah's remembrance of a servant far excels the multiplication of good
deeds. This is further supported by the fact that Allah, Exalted is He, has granted the servant who remembers Him
the reward of his being remembered by Him. In the same
way, the servant who remembers His Messenger ﷺ, is rewarded by his being remembered by Him."

Al-Iraqi said, "Allah's blessing the servant is not his
only reward, for, as we are told in the following *ahadith*, He
also records ten good deeds in the servant's record and re-

moves ten wrong actions from it, and raises him up ten levels."

Anas ibn Malik reported that the Prophet ﷺ said, "If I am mentioned in anyone's presence then he should invoke blessings on me and if anyone invokes blessings on me once, Allah will grant him ten blessings." In another version of this *hadith* the Prophet ﷺ said, "If anyone invokes blessings on me once, Allah will grant him ten blessings, wipe out ten of his wrong actions, and raise him up ten levels." [2]

The Prophet's ﷺ saying, "If I am mentioned in anyone's presence then he should invoke blessings on me", appears to make the invocation of blessings on him ﷺ obligatory in this situation. There is further proof of this in the *hadith*, "The miser is the one in whose presence I am mentioned and yet he does not invoke blessings on me." [3]

Ibn Mas'ud reported that the Messenger of Allah ﷺ said, "Allah has roaming angels who come and inform me of the blessings that my *Ummah* invoke on me." [4]

Ibn Mas'ud also reported that the Messenger of Allah ﷺ said, "The nearest to me on the Day of Resurrection will be those who invoke blessings on me frequently." [5]

It is best to frequently invoke blessings on the Messenger of Allah ﷺ on Fridays. Aws ibn Aws has related that the Messenger of Allah ﷺ said, "Among the most excellent of your days is Friday because on that day Adam was created, and on it he died, and on that day the Trumpet will be sounded, and on it shall come the Hour. So invoke blessings on me frequently on that day, for your blessings will be brought to me." He was asked, "O Messenger of Allah, how will our blessings be conveyed to you when your body has become part of the decaying earth?" He replied, "Allah has prohibited the earth from destroying the bodies of the prophets." [6]

As for the form the invocation of blessings on the Prophet ﷺ should take, Abu Mas'ud Al-Ansari related, "We were sitting in the company of Sa'd ibn Ubada, when the Messenger of Allah ﷺ came to us. Bashir ibn Sa'd said, 'O Messenger of Allah, Allah has commanded us to ask blessings on you but how should we invoke blessings on you?' The Messenger of Allah ﷺ kept silent. We were much perturbed over his silence and wished that he had not asked him this question. Finally, the Messenger of Allah ﷺ said, 'Say, "O Allah, bless Muhammed and the family of Muhammad as You blessed Ibrahim and the family of Ibrahim. O Allah, give *baraka* to Muhammed and the family of Muhammad as You gave *baraka* to Ibrahim and the family of Ibrahim. Surely You are worthy of Praise and Glorious," and then give the *taslim* as you have learnt.'" [7]

Notes

1. Muslim, *Kitab as-Salah*, 4/128.
2. *Sahih*, Ibn as-Sunni, *'Amal al-Yawm wa'l-Laylah*, no. 382. See also Muslim, *Kitab as-Salah*, 4/127.
3. *Sahih*, an-Nisa'i, *Fadha'il al-Qur'an*, no. 125; at-Tirmidhi, *Kitab ad-Da'awat*, 9/531; Ahmad, *al-Musnad*, 1/201; al-Hakim, *Kitab ad-Du'a*, 1/549.
4. *Sahih*, Ahmad, *al-Musnad*, 1/387; an-Nisa'i, *Kitab as-Sahw*, 3/43. Ibn al-Qayim said, "Its *isnad* is *sahih*." See *Jalaa'ul-Afhaam*, p.23.
5. *Hasan*, at-Tirmidhi, *Kitab al-Witr*, 2/607; Ibn Hibban, *Mawarid adh-Dham'an*, p.594.

6. *Sahih,* Ibn Ma'jah, *Kitab al-Jana'iz,* 1/524; Abu Da'wud, *Kitab as-Salah,* 3/370; Ahmad, *al-Fath ar-Rabbani,* 6/9. Al-Hakim said, "It is *sahih,*" in his *Kitab al-Jumu'a,* 1/278.

7. Muslim, *Kitab as-Salat,* 4/123.

TEN

PRAYING AT NIGHT

Allah says:

❮ Surely your Lord knows that you stand (in prayer) two thirds of the night, or a half of it, or a third of it. (73:20) ❯

And also:

❮ And those who spend the night before their Lord, in prostration and standing. (25:64) ❯

The Prophet ﷺ said, "The best prayer, after the obligatory prayers, is the night prayer." [1]

Aisha, may Allah be pleased with her, said, "Between the *'isha* prayer and the *fajr* prayer, the Prophet, may Allah bless him and grant him peace, used to pray eleven *rak'at*. He used to give the *taslim* after every two *rak'at* and then pray one *witr rak'a*." [2']

Ibn Mas'ud related that mention was made before the Prophet ﷺ, of someone who sleeps throughout the night until dawn (without praying). The Prophet ﷺ said, "That is a man in whose ears *shaytan* urinates." [3]

The Prophet ﷺ said, "When any one of you sleeps, *shaytan* ties three knots at the back of your head. On each knot he repeats and exhales the following words, 'The night is long, so stay asleep'. If you wake up and remember Allah, one knot is undone; and if you do *wudu*, the second knot is undone; and if you pray, the third knot is undone, and you get up in the morning full of energy and with a clear heart. Otherwise, you get up feeling lazy and with a muddled heart."4

Ibn Mas'ud used to get up when other people were asleep, and a continuous humming, like the humming of bees, could be heard coming from him until daybreak.

Al-Hasan was once asked, "How is it that those who stay up at night have the most attractive faces?" He replied, "Because they are on intimate terms with the Merciful, and He robes them in some of His light."

He also said, "A man commits a sin and so (because of it) he is deprived of staying up at night."

A man once said to a righteous man, "I am unable to keep on staying up at night; give me a remedy." The righteous man said, "Do not disobey Him during the day and He will keep you up, between His hands, at night."

It has been transmitted that Suffian ath-Thawri said, "I was once deprived of staying up at night for five months because of a sin that I had committed."

Ibn al-Mubarak said:

> When the night is completely dark,
> it finds them staying up in the night.
> Fear has chased away their sleep so they stay up,
> while those who feel secure in this life quietly sleep on.

Abu Sulaiman said, "The people of the night are more content with their staying up at night than the people who play are with their play. Were it not for the night, I would not have liked to continue living in this world."

Ibn Al-Munkadir said, "Only three pleasures remain in this life: staying up at night, meeting one's brothers, and doing the obligatory prayers in *jama'a*."

Notes

1. Muslim, 8/54.
2. Al-Bukhari, *Kitab al-Witr*, 2/478; Muslim, *Kitab al-Musafirin*, 6/16.
3. Al-Bukhari, *Kitab at-Tahajjud*, 3/28; Muslim, *Kitab al-Musafirin*, 6/63.
4. Al-Bukhari, *Kitab at-Tahajjud*, 3/24; Muslim, *Kitab al-Musafirin*, 6/65.

ELEVEN

DOING WITHOUT THE PLEASURES OF THIS WORLD

Abu'l-Abbas as-Sa'idi said, "A man came to the Prophet ﷺ and said, 'O Messenger of Allah! Guide me to such an action that when I do it, Allah will love me and the people will also love me.' He said, 'Be detached from this world and then Allah will love you, and do not be attached to what people have and then the people will love you.'"[1]

This *hadith* shows that Allah loves those who live simply in this life. It has been said that if having love for Allah is the best state to be in, then living simply is the best condition to be in.

Living simply means that you should restrain your desire for worldly things in the hope of receiving something better instead. In order to achieve this more easily you should first realise that the things which people yearn for in this world are in fact worthless when compared with what we hope for in the next world.

If we know that what Allah has will remain and that the life to come is better and more lasting, then we realise that the life of this world is really like a piece of ice left out in the sun – it soon melts and vanishes. The *akhira*, however, essentially never vanishes. The desire one has to exchange this life for the one to come is strengthened by the certainty that there is no comparison between this life and the next.

In the Qur'an we find this world and the next world described in the following terms:

❰ Yes, you prefer the life of this world, but the next world is better and more lasting. (87:16-17) ❱

And also:

❰ You desire the attractions of this world, but Allah desires the next world for you. (8:67) ❱

And also:

❰ And they are happy with the life of this world, but the life of this world is small comfort compared to the next world. (13:26) ❱

The *ahadith* which scorn worldly goods and describe how worthless they are in the sight of Allah are many:

Jabir ibn Abdullah reported that the Messenger of Allah ﷺ happened to walk through the market place. Some people were gathered on either side of him. There he came across a dead goat with very short ears, of which he took hold, saying, "Who among you would like to have this for a *dirham*?" They said, "We would not even like to have it for nothing, for it is of no use to us." He said, "Would you like to have it for free?" They said, "By Allah, not even if it were alive, because its ears are so short; and now it is also dead." Thereupon the Messenger of Allah ﷺ said, "By Allah, this world is more insignificant in the sight of Allah than this is in your eyes." [2]

It has been related by Ibn Shaddad al-Fahri that the Prophet ﷺ said, "This world, in comparison with the world to come, is the same as if one of you were to put his finger in the ocean. Consider how much you would have when you pulled it out." [3]

It has been related by Ibn Sahl ibn Sa'ad that the Prophet ﷺ said, "Had the world been worth even the wing of a gnat to Allah, He would not have even given a drink of water from it to a *kafir*." [4]

Living simply means turning away from the things of this world because they are so worthless. You do not bother with them and remain detached from them.

Yunus ibn Maisarah said, "Being detached from this world does not mean that you should forbid what Allah has permitted, nor that you should squander money. Rather, it is a state in which you are more certain of what is in the hand of Allah than you are of what is in your own hands: your state in misfortune is the same as your state at other times; your attitude towards those who quite rightly criticise you and those who quite rightly praise you is the same."

He has explained this in terms of three stages, or stations, all of which are concerned with the heart rather than with physical action. This is why Abu Sulaiman used to say that you should not call anyone a *zahid*.

The **first** station is that of a servant who is more certain of what is in the hand of Allah than he is of what is in his own hands. This station arises from a healthy and strong conviction.

Abu Hazim az-Zahid was asked, "What is your wealth?" He said, "Two kinds of wealth dispel all fear of poverty: trust in Allah and not being attached to what people have." He was asked, "Don't you fear poverty?" He said, "How can I fear poverty when my Lord owns all that is in the heavens and on the earth and all that is between them and all that is beneath the ground?"

Al-Fudayl said, "The essence of living simply is being content with Allah, Mighty and Exalted is He."

He also said, "The one who is content is the one who lives simply, and it is he who is rich. The one who has attained real faith, who trusts in Allah in all his affairs, and is content with what He provides for him, and remains unattached to the creation, out of fear and hope – and by so doing finds that pursuing worldly gains is not worthwhile – has attained the benefits of simplicity. He is the richest of people, even though he may not possess a thing in the world."

As Ammar said, "Death is teacher enough, true faith is wealth enough, and worship is action enough."

Ibn Mas'ud said, "True belief is not trying to please people by doing things which would bring Allah's displeasure on you; and not envying anyone for what Allah has given him; and not blaming anyone for what Allah has not given you. For Allah's provision is not attracted simply by a man's being careful, nor is it deflected by another man's malice. Allah, with His Justice, Omniscience and Wisdom, has made delight and joy the companions of faith and contentment, and despair and sorrow the companions of distrust and dissatisfaction."

The **second** station is that of a servant who, if he is afflicted by some misfortune – like the death of a child, or the loss of wealth or goods – desires the reward for his accepting the loss more than his recovering what has been lost. This is also a consequence of having complete trust. Ali, may Allah be pleased with him, said, "Whoever lives simply in this world finds misfortunes easy to endure." Some of our predecessors used to say, "If it were not for the misfortunes of this world, we would arrive in the next world completely destitute."

The **third** station is that of a servant who regards praise and criticism equally. If the world occupies a place of importance in his heart, then he would prefer praise to blame, which in turn might make him abandon much good for fear of being censured, and do many bad things in his quest for praise. This means that in his heart other people's opinions about him are of no importance to him – indeed what is important to him is his love of the Truth and his earning Allah's good pleasure.

Ibn Mas'ud said, "True faith is not trying to please other people by doing things which are displeasing to Allah." Allah has praised those who fight in His way, without worrying about the opinions of others. Al-Hasan said, "The person who lives simply is the one who finds it in his heart to say that someone else has surpassed him in it." *Imam* Ahmad, I believe, was once asked whether a wealthy man could live simply. He said, "Yes, if he is not pleased when his wealth increases, nor sad when it decreases, then he can."

Ibrahim ibn Adham said, "There are three types of *zuhud*, or doing without: the first is as a result of having to do so, the second of praiseworthy action, and the third of being careful. Avoiding *haram* things is obligatory, avoiding things which are *halal* may be praiseworthy, and avoiding things which are doubtful is prudent."

Any person who exchanges the things of this world for the next world is doing without something in this life and so we can call him a *zahid*, but doing without can also involve enjoying something in this world at the expense of the next world; in this case it is something in the *akhira* with which one is doing without.

A righteous man was once told, "You do without much more than I do." The man replied, "It is you who are more extreme in this, for I deny myself things in a life which will not last and whose rewards are uncertain, while you have denied yourself the *akhira*. No one could be more extreme in their doing without than this."

Normally, however, when we speak of *zuhud* we mean that we deny ourselves some of the pleasures of this world rather than those of the next world. However it is only possible to abstain from things to which you have access. This is why Ibn al-Mubarak said, when someone said to him, "O *Zahid*!", "The real *zahid* is Umar ibn Abdal-Aziz, for he rejected the tremendous pleasures and riches of this world that were placed at his feet, whereas I have very little to give up."

Al-Hasan al-Basri said, "I have known people and kept company with groups who neither rejoiced when the things of this world came to them, nor grieved when they lost anything in this world. The life of this world was more insignificant to them than dust. One of them might live for a year or for sixty years without ever having a garment that would entirely cover him, and without ever having anything that would come between him and the ground, and without ever having any food that he could ask to be prepared for him in his own home.

"When night came, they would be on their feet, with their foreheads flat against the earth, tears rolling down their cheeks, secretly calling on Allah to save them on the Day of Judgement. If they did something good, they never stopped being grateful for it, and were always asking Allah to accept it. If they did something bad, they would be saddened by it, and would keep on asking Allah to forgive them for it. By Allah, they were not safe from wrong actions, and were saved only by their constant turning in repentance. May Allah be pleased with them and grant them His mercy."

There are three stages of *zuhud*:

The **first** stage is to withdraw from the life of this world, even though you may still have a great desire for it and your heart is still drawn towards it. The self is still preoccupied with the world, even though you struggle with it and restrain it.

The **second** stage is to acquire detachment from this world and to do without in it, in order to obtain your reward for avoiding it. Here, it is your doing without which preoccupies you. This is the state of the person who gives away a *dirham* in order to obtain two.

The **third** stage is that of the one who willingly puts the world to one side without even a thought for what he has abandoned. This is the one who has exchanged a fragment of broken pottery for a jewel.

Or it is like someone who, seeking to gain entrance to see the King, may be prevented by a dog at the gate. By throwing the dog a scrap it is distracted, and this makes it possible for him to gain entrance to the King's audience chamber. *Shaytan* is like that dog, standing at the gates of Allah. He tries to prevent people from entering them, even though the gates are wide open and the world is just a scrap which you can toss aside without a second thought.

Notes

1. *Hasan,* Ibn Ma'jah, *Kitab az-Zuhud,* 2/1373.
2. Muslim, *Kitab az-Zuhud,* 18/93.
3. Muslim, *Kitab al-Jannatu wa Na'imuha,* 17/191.
4. *Sahih gharib,* at-Tirmidhi, *Kitab az-Zuhud,* 6/611.

68

TWELVE

THE STATES OF THE SELF

There is agreement amongst those who seek Allah, despite their different schools and practices, that the self stands between the heart and reaching Him. Only the silencing of the self – by turning away from it and ignoring its whims and overcoming it – can lead you into the domain of Allah and make it possible to reach Him.

There are two kinds of people: one kind are those whose *nafs* have overcome them and led them to ruin because they yielded to them and obeyed their impulses. The other kind are those who have overcome their *nafs* and made them obey their commands.

Some of those who know have said, "The journey of those who seek Allah ends with them overcoming their selves, because whoever triumphs over his self succeeds and wins, and whoever has his self triumph over him loses."

Allah, the Exalted, says:

❨ Then as for whoever exceeded the limits and preferred the life of this world, surely his abode will be the Fire; and as for whoever feared to stand before his Lord and restrained the desires of his self, surely his abode will be the Garden. (79:37-40) ❩

The self urges you to wrong actions, and to preferring this life to the next life; while Allah tells his servants to fear Him, and to restrain the self from following its impulses. The heart is torn between these two. It listens to one caller one moment and to the other caller the next. Here lies the source of affliction, and a challenge.

In the Qur'an, Allah has described three states of the self: the self at peace, the reproachful self, and the self that urges evil. Accordingly, people have varied in their views as to whether a servant has one self, of which these three states are attributes, or three selves.

The first view is that of the people of knowledge and explanation, while the second has been attributed to the Sufis. The truth of the matter is that there is no contradiction between the two. The self is a single entity as far as its essence is concerned, and is one of three main types, depending on what attributes it has.

The Self at Peace

When the self can rest at peace in the Presence of Allah, and is made tranquil when His Name is invoked, and always relates all matters to Him, and often turns to Him, and is impatient to meet Him, and experiences the intimacy of His nearness, then this is a soul at peace. It is the soul to whom it is said at the time of death:

❮ O soul at peace, return to your Lord, well pleased and well-pleasing. Enter with My servants, enter into My Garden. (89:27-30) ❯

Ibn al-Abbas, may Allah be pleased with him, said, "It is the tranquil and believing soul."

Qatada said, "It is the soul of the believer, made calm by what Allah has promised. Its owner is at complete rest and content with his knowledge of Allah's Names and Attributes, and with what He has said about Himself and His Messenger, may Allah bless him and grant him peace, and with what He has said about what awaits the soul after death – about the departure of the soul, the life in the *barzakh*, and the events of the Day of Resurrection which will follow – so much so that a believer such as this can almost see them with his own eyes. So he submits to the will of Allah and surrenders to Him contentedly, never dissatisfied or complaining, and with his faith never wavering. He does not rejoice at his gains, nor do his afflictions make him despair, for he knows that they were decreed long before they happened to him, even before he was created, for Allah says:

❴ No calamity occurs without the permission of Allah; and whoever trusts in Allah, He guides his heart; and Allah knows all things. (64:11) ❵"

Many of our predecessors have said that such a soul belongs to the servant who, when afflicted by misfortune, knows that it is from Allah and accepts it and submits to His will.

The peace that comes with *ihsan* springs from a reassuring familiarity with the decree of Allah, which is reflected in submission, sincerity and worship. No desire, or will, or force of habit, can be given precedence over His will and command; there can be no attraction to anything that contradicts any of His Attributes; and there can be no desire that opposes His decree – and if ever such a thing does happen to such a person, then he simply dismisses it as the whispering of *shaytan*. Indeed he would rather fall from the sky than give reality to such a thing within himself.

This, as the Prophet ﷺ said, is clear and true faith.[1] By it he is saved from the worry that accompanies wrong actions and from any anxiety about them, thanks to the peace and sweetness that come with turning to Him.

If he comes to rest in firm belief after having doubted, or in knowledge after ignorance, or in remembrance after being forgetful, or in repentance after rebellion, or in sincerity after showing off, or in truthfulness after deceit, or in clarity after confusion, or in the humility of intimacy after the impetuousness of desire, or in modesty after boastfulness, then his soul is at peace.

All this is due to the awareness that frees the heart from idle sleep and lights up the palaces of the Garden ahead of him – as when a man cried out:

> O soul, watch out! Help me with your striving
> in the darkness of the nights,
> so that on the Day of Resurrection
> you will win a good life on those heights!

He recognised, by the light of this awakening, what he had been created for, and what he would encounter, from the moment he died to the moment he entered the abode that lasts for ever (i.e. the Garden or the Fire). He realised how swiftly this world passes, and how unreliable it is for its children, and how it destroys whoever loves it. So he arose in this light, full of determination and said:

❬ Ah, woe is me, that I was forgetful of Allah! (39:56) ❭

So he sets out on a fresh start in his life, making up for what he has missed and bringing back to life what had died. Now he faces the pitfalls that he encountered before head-on, and seizes the moment with his newly discovered capacity, which, when it passed him by before, caused him to miss all good.

Then he realises, in the light of this awakening and in the light of Allah's gifts to him, that he is incapable of measuring and counting Allah's blessings, or of repaying his debt. With this realisation, he recognises his shortcomings and faults, his wrong actions and all the bad things he has done, all of his disobedience and the neglect of so many rights and duties. His self is broken and his body is humbled and he approaches Allah with his head down. He recognises Allah's generosity and sees his own misdeeds and faults both at the same time.

He also sees, in the light of this awakening, how precious his time is, and how important it is. He realises that it is the capital of his future well-being which must not be wasted, and he becomes so thrifty with it that he only spends it in actions and deeds which will bring him nearer to Allah – for wasting time is the seed of failure and regret, and being careful with it is the root of success and joy.

These then, are the consequences of being aware and what increase it. These are the first steps of the soul at peace on its journey to Allah and the *akhira*.

The Reproachful Self

It has been said that this kind of self is the one which cannot rest in any one state. It often changes and alters, remembers and forgets, submits and evades, loves and hates, rejoices and becomes sad, accepts and rejects, obeys and rebels.

It has also been said that it is the self of the believer. Al-Hasan al-Basri said, "You always see the believer reproaching himself and saying things like: 'Did I want this? Why did I do that? Was this better than that?'"

It has also been said that the self blames itself on the Day of Resurrection: every one blames himself for his actions, either for his bad deeds, if he was one who had many wrong actions, or for his short comings, if he was one who did good deeds.

Imam Ibn al-Qayyim says that all of this is accurate.

There are two types of reproachful self: one that is blameworthy and one that is not blameworthy. The blameworthy self is the ignorant, disobedient self that Allah and His angels blame. The self that is not blameworthy is the self that blames its owner for his own shortcomings in obeying Allah, in spite of all his efforts in that direction. This self is not really blameworthy.

The most praiseworthy selves are the ones that blame themselves because of their shortcomings in obeying Allah. This is the self that endures criticism from others in its quest to please Him, so that no one can find fault with it as regards his worship of Him. This one has escaped being blamed by Allah.

As for the self which accepts its actions as they are, without self-criticism, and which does not have to endure the criticisms of others – which means that it cannot be being sincerely obedient to Allah – this is the self that Allah blames.

The Self that Urges Evil

This is the self that brings punishment on itself. By its very nature it directs its owner towards every wrong action. No one can be rid of its evil without help from Allah. As Allah says of the wife of al-Aziz, in the story of Yusuf:

❨ And I do not say that my self is free from blame: surely the self urges evil, unless my Lord is Merciful; surely my Lord is Forgiving, Compassionate. (12:53) ❩

Allah also says:

❨ And had it not been for the grace of Allah and His Mercy on you, not one of you would ever have been pure; but Allah purifies whomever He wishes, and Allah is Hearing, Knowing. (24:21) ❧

We have been taught the *du'a*, "All praise is for Allah, we praise Him and seek His help and His pardon. We seek refuge in Him from the evil in our selves and from the evil of our deeds." [2]

Evil lies hiding in the self, and it is this that leads it on to do wrong. If Allah were to leave the servant alone with his self, the servant would be destroyed between its evil and the evil that it craves; but if Allah grants him success and help, then he will survive. We seek refuge in Allah the Almighty, both from the evil of our selves and from the evil of our deeds.

So the self is a single entity, although its state may change: from the self that urges evil, *an-nafs al-ammara* , to the reproachful self, *an-nafs al-lawwama*, to the self at peace, *an-nafs al-mutma'inna*, which is the final aim of perfection.

The self at peace has an angel to help it, who assists and guides it. The angel casts good into the self, so that it desires what is good and is aware of the excellence of good actions. The angel also keeps the self away from wrong action and shows it the ugliness of bad deeds. All in all, whatever is for Allah and by Him, always comes from the soul which is at peace.

The self which urges evil has *shaytan* as its ally. He promises it great rewards and gains, but casts falsehood into it. He invites it and entices it to do evil. He leads it on with hope after hope and presents falsehood to it in a form that it will accept and admire.

The *nafs al-mutma'inna*, the self at peace, and its angel require the following: unwavering belief in Allah, the One, without any partner; moral excellence; good behaviour towards Allah, and parents, and companions, and so on; fear of Allah; total reliance on Allah; turning in repentance to Allah; relating all things to Allah; drawing near to Allah; curbing expectations; and being prepared for death and what follows it.

Shaytan and his helpers, on the other hand, require the *nafs al-ammara*, the self that urges evil – the opposite of all this.

The most difficult challenge to the self at peace is to free itself from the influence of *shaytan* and the *nafs al-ammara*. If it undertakes this struggle, then it becomes *nafs al-lawwama*, the reproachful self; and if the struggle is won, then it becomes *nafs al-mutma'inna*. If even one good action were to be accepted by Allah, one would have success by virtue of it, but *shaytan* and the *nafs al-ammara* refuse to urge the self to do even one such deed.

Some of those who were given knowledge of Allah and of their own selves have said, "If I could know for certain that even one of my actions had been accepted by Allah, then I would be happier at the arrival of death than the much travelled wayfarer is at the sight of his family." Abdullah ibn Umar said, "If I could know for certain that Allah had accepted even one of my prostrations, there would be no long lost friend dearer to me than death itself."

The *nafs al-ammara* urges evil and openly opposes the *nafs al-mutma'inna*. Whenever the latter presents a good deed, the former presents an evil deed in return. The *nafs al-ammara* tells the *nafs al-mutma'inna* that *jihad* is nothing more than suicide, a widowed wife, orphaned children, and wasted wealth. It tries to convince the *nafs al-mutma'inna* that *zakat* and *sadaqa* are nothing less than an unnecessary expense and a burden, a hole in your pocket, which will lead you to depend on others, so that you too will then be like the poor.

Bringing the Self to Account

When the self that urges evil overwhelms the heart of a believer, the only remedy is to bring it to account and then to disregard it. *Imam* Ahmad has related on the authority of Umar ibn al-Khattab, may Allah be pleased with him, that the Prophet, may Allah bless him and grant him peace, said, "The intelligent person is the one who brings his self to account and acts in preparation for what lies beyond his death; and the foolish person is the one who abandons himself to his desires and cravings and expects Allah to fulfil his futile wishes." [3]

Imam Ahmad also related that Umar Ibn al-Khattab, may Allah be pleased with him, said, "Judge your selves before you yourselves are judged; and weigh your selves in the balance before you yourselves are weighed in the balance. When you are brought to account tomorrow, it will be much easier for you if you have already brought your selves to account today – so do so, before you come to the Final Gathering for:

❨ On that Day you will be exposed – whatever you have hidden will no longer be hidden. (69:18) ❩" [4]

Al-Hasan said, "A believer is responsible for his self, and he brings it to account in order to please Allah. Judgement will be lighter on the Day of Judgement for the people who have brought their selves to account in this life, but it will be severe for the people who did not prepare for it by bringing their selves to account beforehand."

A believer is distracted by something that he likes, so he says to it: "By Allah, I like you and I need you, but there is no means by which I can have you, so you have been kept from me." When whatever it is, is out of his sight and beyond his reach, then he returns to his senses and says, "I did not really want this! What made me preoccupied with it? By Allah, I shall never concern myself with it again!"

The believers are a people who have been prevented through the Qur'an from indulging in the pleasures of this world; it comes between them and what might destroy them. The believer is like a prisoner in this world, who tries to free himself from its shackles and fetters, placing his trust in nothing in it, until the day he meets his Creator. He knows full well that he is accountable for everything that he hears, sees and says, and for everything that he does with his body. [5]

Malik ibn Dinar said, "May Allah grant mercy to a servant who says to his self, 'Aren't you such and such? Didn't you do such and such?' Then he rebukes it and puts it in its place, and disciplines it and restrains it in accordance with the Book of Allah, Mighty and Glorious is He, and becomes its guide and master."

It is undoubtedly the responsibility of anyone who believes in Allah and the Day of Judgement, and who wishes to keep his affairs in order, to make sure that he brings his self to account. He must control what it does and what it does not do, even its most insignificant activities, for each and every breath you take during your life-time is precious. It can be used to acquire one of the treasures which ensure a state of bliss that is everlasting. Whoever wastes it, or uses it to acquire things which may cause his destruction, will suffer great losses, which are only allowed to happen by the most ignorant, foolish and reckless of people. The true extent of such losses will only become apparent on the Day of Judgement. Allah, Exalted is He, says:

❨ On the Day when every soul will be confronted with all the good that it has done and all the evil that it has done, it will wish that there were a great distance between it and its evil. (3:30) ❩

There are two ways of bringing the self to account: one precedes action, the other follows it.

The **first** way is the decision that is made when a believer hesitates before acting. This is the moment of evaluation before intention is formed. He does not proceed until he is sure that it is good and sound. If it is not, then he abandons it.

Al-Hasan, may Allah be pleased with him, said, "May Allah grant mercy to a servant who hesitates at the point of evaluation, and then if he sees that the action is for Allah, he carries on with it, but if he sees that it for something other than Allah, then he holds back from completing it." [6]

This has been explained as meaning that when the self first feels like doing something or other, and the servant begins by considering its worth, he first stops and thinks to himself, "Can I do this?" If the answer is no, he will not undertake the action. If it is yes, he will again stop and ask himself, "Is it better for me to do it than not to do it?" If the answer is no, he will abandon it and not attempt to do it, but if the answer is yes, he will then pause for a third time and ask himself, "Is this action motivated by the desire to seek Allah's pleasure and reward, or is it in order to acquire power, admiration, and money?"

If it is the latter that has prompted the idea of the action, then he will not undertake it, even if it would result in his acquiring those worldly gains which prompted the idea of the action in the first place – for otherwise this would result in his self becoming accustomed to associating others with Allah, and it would make acting for the sake of something or someone other than Allah easier for it, and the easier it is to do things for other than Him, the harder it becomes to do things that are intended for His pleasure.

If it is the former that has prompted the idea of the action, he stops yet again and asks himself, "Will I receive help in doing this? Do I have any companions who will help me and come to my assistance if I need their help in undertaking this action?" If he finds that he has no allies to help him, he will hold back from going through with this action, just as the Prophet ﷺ held back from waging the *jihad* against the Makkans until he had enough allies and sufficient forces to ensure success.

If he finds that there is assistance on which he can rely in undertaking the proposed action, then at last he should start doing it, and he will succeed, by the will of Allah. Failure can only occur if one of these safeguards is lacking, for when they are all combined together they guarantee success. These are the four steps that a servant needs to take in bringing his self to account before he does anything.

The **second** way is that of bringing the self to account after an action. There are three categories of this:

First, bringing the self to account for an act of obedience in which what is due to Allah has not been completely fulfilled or done in the best possible way. There are six things that are due to Allah in acts of obedience:

Sincerity in doing it, devoting it to Allah only, following the example of the Prophet ﷺ, paying attention to doing it well, recognising Allah's blessings in it, and, after all this, being aware of your own shortcomings in how you do it. A person brings his self to account, but has he given all these prerequisites their due attention and effort? Did he fulfill them in his act of obedience?

Second, bringing the self to account for any action which would have been better left undone than done.

Third, bringing the self to account as to whether or not the intention in undertaking a permitted action was to seek the pleasure of Allah, Exalted is He, and success in the *akhira*, thereby guaranteeing success – or was it in fact to seek the fleeting gains of this life, thereby losing what could have otherwise been gained?

The last thing a person should do is to be inattentive and neglectful in bringing his self to account, by starting out without any preparation, and by treating matters lightly and just muddling along. This will only bring about his ruin. This is the destiny of the people who are arrogant.

Such a one turns a blind eye to the consequences of acting like this and relies on Allah's forgiveness. He neglects bringing his self to account and does not contemplate the outcome of his behaviour. If he does not do this, then he easily falls into wrong actions, until he becomes accustomed to them, and then finds it difficult to pull himself away from them.

All in all, the believer should first bring his self to account as regards his obligatory acts of worship. If he finds himself lacking in these, then he should hasten to rectify his situation, either by catching up with the worship he has neglected, or by correcting whatever he may have been doing wrong in his worship.

Next, he he should bring his self to account as regards acts which are forbidden. If he finds that he has done any of them, he must quickly turn in repentance, seek Allah's forgiveness, and do good deeds in order to eradicate the bad deeds which have been recorded in his record.

Next, he he should bring his self to account as regards those matters in which he has been negligent. If he finds that he has been negligent in doing what he was created for, he should hasten to the remembrance of Allah and drawing near to Him with an open heart.

Next, he should bring his self to account for the words he has spoken, for the steps his feet have taken, for the things his hands have grasped, and for what his ears have listened to. He should ask himself, "What did I want this for? What did I do that for? Whom did I do this for? Why did I do it like that?"

He should know that every action and every word are accounted for in two books; one is entitled, "For whom did I do it?", and the other, "How well did I do it?" The first question is concerned with sincerity, and the second is concerned with the action itself. Allah, the Exalted, says:

❰ That He may question the truthful about their truthfulness. (33:8) ❱

If the truthful ones are going to be asked about their truthfulness, and will be judged in accordance with how truthful they were, what do you imagine will be the case with the people of falsehood?

The Merits of Bringing the Soul to Account

This involves:

First, identifying the faults of the self. Whoever does not recognise his faults cannot possibly get rid of them. Yunus ibn Ubaid said, "I know about a hundred of the attributes of goodness and yet I cannot find even one of them in my self."

Muhammed ibn Wasi said, "If wrong actions produced flatulence, no one would have been able to sit in my company."

Imam Ahmad wrote that Abu'd-Darda' said, "No man gains full understanding and knowledge unless he detests all the people who are not close to Allah, and then turns his attention to his own self and detests it even more."

Second, knowing what rights are due to Allah. This is important because it makes the servant detest his self and frees him from arrogance and being self-satisfied with his actions. This opens the doors of submission and humility for him, and results in the purification of his soul at the hands of his Lord. He despairs for his self and believes firmly that his survival will not be achieved without the forgiveness, generosity and mercy of Allah. It is His right to be constantly obeyed, remembered and thanked.

Notes

1. Muslim, *Kitab al-Iman*, 2/153; related on the authority of Abu Huraira, who said, "Some of the companions of the Prophet, may Allah bless him and grant him peace, came to him and said, 'We have found something in our hearts which we are proud to speak about.' He asked them, 'Have you really found it?' They said, 'Yes.' Then he said, 'That is true faith.'"
2. *Sahih hadith*, Abu Da'wud, *Kitab an-Nikah*, 6/153; Ibn Ma'jah, *Kitab an-Nikah*, 1/609.
3. *Da'if*, at-Tirmidhi, *Kitab Sifat al-Qiyyamah*, 7/155; al-Hakim, *al-Mustadrak*, *Kitab al-Iman*, 1/57.
4. Ahmad, *Kitab az-Zuhud*, 7/156; al-Baghawi, *Sharh as-Sunnah*, 14/309; Abu Na'im, *al-Hilya*, 1152.

5. See Ibn Kathir, *al-Bidaya wa'n-Nihaya*, 9/272; Abu Na'im, *al-Hilya*, 2/157.

6. This saying is supported by a *sahih hadith* transmitted by Muslim, *Kitab al-Iman*, 2/18, on the authority of Abu Huraira, who said that the Prophet, may Allah bless him and grant him peace, said, "Let whoever believes in Allah and the Last Day either speak good or keep silent; and let whoever believes in Allah and the Last Day be generous to his neighbour; and let whoever believes in Allah and the Last Day be generous to his guest."

THIRTEEN

PERSEVERANCE

Allah has made perseverance a tireless horse, a relentless cutting sword, an invincible, victorious army, an indestructible, formidable fortress. It and victory are inseparable companions.

Allah, Mighty and Glorious is He, has praised those who persevere in His Book, and says that He gives them endless rewards and supports them with His guidance, might and a clear victory. He says:

❨ And be patient – surely Allah is with those who are patient. (8:46) ❩

By virtue of this companionship, those who persevere gain both in this life and in the next life as they deserve; they win both His evident and hidden blessings.

Allah has made leadership in the *deen* dependent on perseverance and certainty. He says:

❨ And We appointed leaders from among them who guided by Our command, so long as they persevered and firmly believed in Our Signs. (32:24) ❩

And He says that the perseverance of those who persevere is good for them, and He has affirmed this with an oath:

❨ And if you persevere, that is indeed better for those who persevere. (16:126) ❩

And He says that through perseverance and fear of Allah, the schemes of the enemy will not cause His faithful servants any harm, even if they are of the worst kind:

❨ And if you persevere and have *taqwa*, their cunning will not harm you at all – surely Allah surrounds whatever they do. (3:120) ❩

Allah has made success conditional on perseverance and righteousness:

❨ O you who believe, persevere, and be patient, and hold together firmly, and fear Allah, so that you may be successful. (3:200) ❩

He also speaks of His love for those who persevere, which is the greatest incentive possible for anyone who seeks His love:

❨ And Allah loves those who persevere. (3:146) ❩

Allah gives good news to those who persevere and promises them three things, each of which is far better than anything the people of this world envy one another for:

❨ And give good news to those who persevere, those who say, when a misfortune strikes them, "Surely we come from Allah, and surely to Him we return"; these are the ones on whom blessings from their Lord descend, and mercy, and these are the ones who are rightly guided. (2:155-157) ❩

Allah has made the attainment of a place in the Garden and the avoidance of a place in the Fire the exclusive reward of those who patiently persevere:

❨ Surely I have rewarded them this Day for their patience and surely they are the ones who are successful (23:111) ❩

By making them the particular beneficiaries of His *ayat*, Allah has distinguished those who endure and persevere and are grateful for such great good fortune. He says, in four different places in the Qur'an:

❨ Surely in this there are signs for every one who perseveres and gives thanks. (14:5, 31:31, 34:19 and 42:33) ❩

Perseverance is a true attribute of the believer. He circles round it and then returns to it. It is the pillar that supports his faith, without which he could not remain upright. Whoever has no perseverance can have no faith, or if he does have some faith, then it is scant and weak. Such a person worships Allah half-heartedly: if he encounters good in this life, he is reassured in his belief, but if he is afflicted by misfortune, then he turns away from Allah and loses everything both in this life and in the next life, settling for a losing deal.

The good news proclaimed by the Prophet Jesus, peace be on him, was only appreciated by the fortunate ones because of their perseverance, and they ascended to the highest ranks because of their gratitude. They flew with the wings of perseverance and gratitude to the Gardens of Bliss:

❨ Race with each other towards forgiveness from your Lord and a Garden whose extent is like the extent of the heavens and the earth which is in store for those who believe in Allah and His messengers. That is Allah's grace which He grants to whomever He wishes – and Allah's grace is vast. (57:21) ❩

Since perseverance and gratitude are two elements of faith, whoever is concerned about the well being of his soul – desiring its salvation and hoping for its good fortune – must not neglect these two essentials.

He must approach Allah with them, so that He may put him among those who are successful on the Day that he meets Him.

The Meaning and Essence of Perseverance

The word *sabr* in Arabic, meaning 'perseverance' or 'patience', indicates holding back and self-restraint. In the context of the *shari'ah*, it means keeping the self from being agitated, the tongue from complaining, and the hands from beating cheeks and tearing clothes (as an expression of grief).

It has been said that it is one of the excellent possessions of the self, without which it is not possible to do anything well. It is a strength of the self that makes it possible to put it right and benefit it.

When *Imam* Junaid was asked what it is, he said, "Swallowing something bitter without displaying any distaste on your face."

Dhu'n-Nun al-Misri said of it, "Perseverance is distancing yourself from all wrongs and transgressions, and remaining calm when you are engulfed by impossible afflictions, and appearing to have enough when poverty is in permanent residence in your home."

It has also been said that perseverance is, "Standing firm and remaining courteous when affliction strikes, and remaining content when afflicted with misfortune, without showing any signs of complaint."

One day, a righteous man saw someone complaining to his brother, so he said to him, "By Allah – what you are really doing is complaining about the One Who is merciful to you, as you complain to one who has no mercy of his own to give to you."

It has also been said:

When you complain to the son of Adam,
you are in fact complaining about the Merciful
to one who has no mercy of his own.

There are two types of complaint:

The **first** type of complaint is a complaining to Allah, Mighty and Glorious is He, which is not inconsistent with perseverance, as in the saying of the Prophet Ya'qub, peace be on him, when he said:

❴ "I only reveal my distress and sorrow to Allah." (12:86) ❵

And also:

❴ "So patience is beautiful." (12:83) ❵

The Prophet ﷺ said, "O Allah! I complain to You about the weakness of my strength and the lack of my ability." [1]

The **second** type of complaint is a complaining about affliction, by objecting to its nature and character. This kind is incompatible with perseverance and it contradicts it and cancels it out.

The arena of power is more significant for the servant than the arena of perseverance; as the Prophet ﷺ said to Allah, "If You are not angry with me, I will not be concerned, but Your Might is more significant for me." [2]

This does not contradict his ﷺ saying, "No one has been given a better or greater gift than perseverance." [3]

This applies to someone who has been afflicted by a misfortune. The arena of perseverance in his case is the greatest one, but, before affliction strikes, the arena of strength and health is more significant.

The self is the riding beast that carries the servant either to the Garden or to the Fire. Perseverance is to the self what the reins and blinkers are to the riding beast – if it had neither, it would wander off in all directions.

Al-Hajjaj once said, "Keep your selves in check, for they can get up to all sorts of mischief. May Allah grant mercy to whom-ever puts reins and blinkers on his self, directing it with the blinkers towards obedience to Allah, and steering it away from disobedience with the reins. Patiently avoiding what Allah has forbidden is easier than enduring the punishment that He inflicts."

There are two types of impetus that drive the self: one is the active impulse of courage, and the other is the inhibiting force of restraint.

The true essence of perseverance is to chanel the first type of energy towards what is beneficial, and to use the second type of energy to avoid doing what is harmful.

There are people who persevere in doing the night prayer regularly and in enduring the burden of fasting, and yet they do not have the power to refrain from a forbidden glance. There are others who can do this, and yet they do not have the energy to persevere in enjoining good and forbidding evil, or in fighting a *jihad*.

It has been said, "Endurance, patience, and perseverance are what constitute the bravery of the self." Similar to this saying is the proverb, "Courage is being able to persevere for a while."

Enduring patiently is the opposite of being agitated. As Allah, Mighty and Glorious is He, says of the people of the Fire and what they say:

❨ Whether we rage, or patiently endure, is the same for us (now) – for us there is no way of escape. (14:21) ❩

Types of Perseverence

There are three kinds of perseverance, depending on the intention behind it: perseverance in completing acts of worship and being obedient; perseverance in refraining from forbidden actions and being disobedient; and perseverance in the face of destiny so that the servant does not become angry in times of adversity.

It has been said about these different types, "A servant must have a command to obey, prohibitions to avoid, and adversity to endure."

There is another way of categorising endurance and perseverance, namely, perseverance where there is a choice and perseverance where there is no choice. The former is better and has greater significance than the latter, for perseverance where there is no choice is the kind which is common to all people; it is exercised by all those who do not display perseverance by choice.

For this reason the perseverance of the Prophet Yusuf, peace be on him, in refusing the advances of the wife of al-Aziz is more significant than his enduring what his brothers inflicted on him when they threw him in the well.

Man can never do without perseverance. He fluctuates between a command that he must obey and fulfil, prohibitions he must avoid and do without, destiny which must run its course, and blessings for which he must thank the Provider. As the human situation never changes, man has to persevere until the day he dies.

Everything that the servant meets in this life is one of two kinds: one kind matches his desires and accords with his wishes, while the other does not.

He needs to have patience for both kinds, but the first kind – such as having health, wealth and power – requires more patience from him in several respects:

First, he should not place his confidence in them; nor should he be arrogant and bad mannered because of them; nor should they be the cause of his being ungrateful; nor should he celebrate with them in ways of which Allah does not approve.

Second, he should not become preoccupied with acquiring them.

Third, he must persevere in fulfilling what is due to Allah in them.

Fourth, he must persist in his efforts not to expend them in making *haram* profits.

It has been said, "Both the *mumin* and the *kafir* are able to persevere in times of hardship, but only the truly faithful are capable of persevering in times of ease."

Abdur-Rahman ibn Awf said, "We were afflicted with hardship, and we persevered and endured, but when we enjoyed times of ease, we were unable to persevere." That is why Allah warns His servants against becoming engrossed or preoccupied with money, spouses and children. He says, Mighty and Exalted is He:

❨ O you who believe, do not let your wealth or your children distract you from the remembrance of Allah. (63:9) ❩

The other kind, which does not accord with his desires and wishes, is either related to matters where the servant has a choice – such as acts of obedience or disobedience – or with matters in which the servant has no choice – such as afflictions. Perhaps he has a choice in the very beginning, but not in ending them once they are under way.

Thus of this second kind there are three categories:

First, there are matters in which the servant has a choice, which include all the actions involving either obedience or disobedience.

In the case of actions involving obedience, the servant needs to persevere in doing them because the self, by its very nature, dislikes much of what is involved in worship and service. In doing the prayer, for example, the self is lazy and prefers taking it easy, especially if it is accompanied by a hardened heart that has been overwhelmed by wrong action, and is inclined to follow its own desires and mix with people who neglect Allah's commands. In paying *zakat*, perseverance and endurance are needed because of the mean and miserly characteristics of the self. In doing the *hajj* and fighting *jihad*, perseverance is required, because of both of the above mentioned characteristics combined: laziness and meanness.

A servant needs to persevere in three circumstances:

First, before fulfilling an act of obedience, by paying attention to his sincerity in doing this act of obedience.

Second, during the act of obedience, by persisting in completing it without any omissions and without being negligent, in accordance with his sincere intentions, and without allowing the physical performance of the action to distract his heart from being at rest in full submission before Allah, the Exalted.

Third, after completing the act of obedience by patiently avoiding anything that might wipe out its reward. This kind of patience means that he must not be pleased with his having been obedient and boast about it, bringing it out from the realm of the veiled secret in to that of public scrutiny.

The act of the servant is a secret between himself and Allah, the Exalted, and it is recorded as such in the realm of secrets. If he talks about it, it is removed from there to the realm of public knowledge. So he must not think that there is no more need for perseverance once the physical action has been completed.

In the case of acts of disobedience, the matter is clear and simple. The greatest help for the servant in patiently avoiding such acts is to give up his bad habits and to avoid contact with those who encourage such habits through companionship and conversation.

Second, there are matters in which the servant has no choice, and which he has no means of avoiding, such as misfortunes, which either are not of man's own making – like death and illness – or are caused by man – like physical violence and verbal abuse.

In relation to the first kind of misfortune, there are four known stations: the station of inability to cope, which includes being agitated and complaining; the station of patient endurance and perseverance; the station of acceptance and contentment; and the station of gratitude, in which the misfortune is viewed as a blessing – and so the one who is afflicted is thankful to the One Who Afflicts him for it.

In relation to the second kind of misfortune, which is caused by man, there are these four stations, plus four more: the station of forgiveness; the station of clarity of the heart regarding any wish to satisfy any desire for revenge; the station of being in a position to do so; and the station of treating the wrongdoer with kindness.

Third, there are matters which are brought about by the servant's own choice, but once they have happened and taken hold of his situation, he is left with no choice in being able to change them or to free himself from their effects on him.

The Merits of Perseverance

Umm Salama, may Allah be pleased with her, reported that she heard the Messenger of Allah 鸞 say, "There is no Muslim who, when afflicted with a misfortune, says as Allah has ordered him to say, ❴ Surely to Allah we belong, and surely to Him we are returning, (2:156) ❵ O Allah, reward me in my misfortune and give me better than it afterwards', except that Allah grants him better than it."

She continued, "When Abu Salama died, I said, 'Which one of the Muslims is better than Abu Salama, whose family was the first to follow the Messenger of Allah 鸞 in making *hijra*?' Then I said what Allah has ordered us to say, and He gave me marriage to His Messenger 鸞." [4]

Abu Huraira has related that the Messenger of Allah 鸞 said, "The Mighty and Glorious says, 'I have nothing but the Garden as a reward for My faithful servant who, when I take back one of the most excellent people of this world (i.e. through death), remains patient and hopes for Allah's reward.'" [5]

In the two books of *as-Sahih*, it is reported that Aisha, may Allah be pleased with her, related that the Messenger of Allah 鸞 said, "Any believer who is afflicted by a misfortune, even if it is as little as the prick of a thorn, will have it removed from his record of wrong actions, in return for it." [6]

Abu Huraira reported that the Prophet 鸞 said, "The believer continues to be afflicted with hardships in his or her body, wealth and children, until he or she meets Allah completely free of all wrong actions." [7]

Khabbab ibn al-Arath reported, "We complained to the

Messenger of Allah ﷺ about our situation while he was lying in the shade of the Ka'aba, with his head resting on his cloak. We said, 'Will you ask Allah to help us? Will you invoke Allah for us?'

"He said, 'Among those who were before you, a believer used to be seized and placed in a pit dug especially for him; then a saw would be brought and put on his head which would then be cut into two halves, after his flesh had been sliced with iron combs and torn from his bones – and yet all that did not make him abandon his *deen*. By Allah! this *deen* will be completed, and a rider will be able to travel from San'a to Hadramout, fearing nobody except Allah and the wolf – lest it should trouble his sheep – but you are impatient!'" [8]

Some of our predecessors used to say, "Had it not been for misfortunes, we would have arrived in the *akhira* completely destitute."

Sufyan ibn 'Uyaynah, when commenting on the following *ayah* of the Qur'an:

❨ And We appointed leaders from among them who guided by Our command, so long as they persevered and firmly believed in Our signs. (32:24) ❩

said, "When they wanted to amputate Urwah ibn az-Zubair's leg, they said to him, 'Shall we give you a drink so that you won't feel the pain?' He replied, 'Allah has given me this affliction in order to test my endurance – shall I then act against His will?'"

Umar ibn Abdal-Aziz said, "Whenever Allah gives a blessing to a servant, and then takes it back from him, and the servant patiently endures his loss, then He rewards him with a blessing which is better than the one which He took back."

When Abu Bakr as-Siddiq, may Allah be pleased with him, fell ill and people visited him, they said to him, "Shouldn't we call a doctor to see you?" He said, "The Doctor has already seen me." They said, "What did He say to you?" He said, "'Whatever I wish, I make it happen.'"

It has been related that Sa'id ibn Jubair said, "Perseverance is the servant's acceptance before Allah of the affliction that He has caused to befall him, his recognition that Allah has taken it into account, and his hope that Allah will reward him for it. The servant may inwardly be in a state of fright and panic, but by exercising his self-control, nothing but perseverance can be observed in his demeanour."

Ibn Jubair's saying, "the servant's acceptance before Allah of the affliction that He has caused to befall him", is like an explanation of the words, "Surely to Allah we belong". Here, the servant accepts that he belongs to Allah and that Allah does as He wishes with His possessions.

His saying, "his hope that Allah will reward him for it", is like an explanation of the words, "and surely to Him we are returning". It means that when we return to our Lord, He rewards us for our perseverance – for the reward for perseverance is never lost.

Notes

1. *Da'if*, al-Haythami, *Majma' az-Zawa'id*, 6/35.
2. *Da'if*, part of the previous *hadith*.
3. Al-Bukhari, *Kitab az-Zakat*, 3/335; Muslim, *Kitab az-Zakat*, 7/144.
4. Muslim, *Kitab al-Jana'iz*, 6/220.

5. Al-Bukhari, *Kitab ar-Riqaq*, 11/241.

6. Al-Bukhari, *Kitab al-Mardha*, 10/111; Muslim, *Kitab al-Birr wa's-Silah*, 16/129.

7. Ahmad, *al-Musnad*, 2/287; at-Tirmidhi, *Kitab az-Zuhud*, 7/80; al-Hakim, *Kitab ar-Riqaq*, 4/124.

8. Al-Bukhari, *Kitab al-Ikrah*, 12/315, and also *Kitab Manaqib al-Ansar*, 7/164.

FOURTEEN

GRATITUDE

Gratitude is thanking the One who grants blessings for His generosity. The gratitude of a servant should have three qualities, without which it can hardly be considered to be gratitude. They are the inner recognition and appreciation of the blessing, speaking about it openly, and using it as a means to worshipping Him.

Gratitude is a matter for the heart, the tongue and the limbs. The heart is for knowledge and love of Him; the tongue is for thanking and praising Him; and the limbs are to be used in obeying the One Who is being thanked, and in holding back from committing disobedient acts.

Allah, Glorious and Exalted is He, has linked gratitude with belief. He says that He does not need to punish His creatures if they thank Him and believe in Him. He says:

❨ What has Allah to do with punishing you, if you are grateful and you believe? (4:147) ❩

The Glorious and Mighty also says that the people who are grateful are singled out from the rest of His servants because of the mercy that He displays towards them. The Mighty and Glorious says:

❨ And thus We test some of them by means of others, so that they say, "Are these the ones whom Allah has favoured from amongst us?" Is not Allah best Aware of those who give thanks? (6:53) ❩

He divides people into those who are grateful and those who are ungrateful; and the most displeasing thing to Him is ingratitude and its people; and the most precious thing to Him is gratitude and its people:

❰ Surely We have shown him the way, whether he is grateful or ungrateful. (76:3) ❱

And also:

❰ And when your Lord proclaimed: "If you are thankful, I will give you more, but if you are ungrateful, then surely My punishment is terrible indeed." (14:7) ❱

In these *ayat*, Allah makes the granting of more blessings conditional on gratitude. There is no limit to the increase in His blessings, just as there is no limit to being grateful to Him. Allah, Mighty and Glorious is He, has made a great deal of reward dependent on His will. He says:

❰ And if you fear poverty, Allah will enrich you through His generosity, if He wills. Surely Allah is Knowing, Wise. (9:28) ❱

And also:

❰ And He forgives whomever He wills. (5:40) ❱

And also:

❰ And Allah turns in mercy towards whomever He wills. (9:15) ❱

He puts no limit on His reward for gratitude when He refers to it:

❰ We shall reward those who are thankful. (3:145) ❱

When the enemy of Allah, *shaytan*, learned of the value of gratitude – and that it is one of the most exalted and highest states – he directed his efforts towards distancing people from it:

❨ "Then will I approach them from in front of them and from behind them, and from their right and from their left; and You will find that most of them are not grateful." (7:17) ❩

Allah has described the grateful ones among His worshippers as being few in number:

❨ And only a few of My servants are grateful. (34:13) ❩

The Prophet ﷺ is reported to have stayed up in prayer all night until his feet swelled up. He was asked, "Why do you do this when Allah has already forgiven you all your past and future wrong actions?" He, may Allah bless him and grant him peace, said, "Should I not still be a grateful servant?" [1]

The Prophet ﷺ once told Mu'adh, "By Allah, you are dear to me! So do not forget to say at the end of each prayer, "O Allah, help me in remembering You, in being grateful to You and in serving You well." [2]

Gratitude is linked to Allah's generosity and it is what makes it increase. Umar ibn Abdal-Aziz said, "Join Allah's generosity towards you to your gratitude towards Him."

Ibn Abi'd-Dunya reported that Ali ibn Abi Talib, may Allah be pleased with him, said to a man from the tribe of Hamazan, "Allah's generosity is connected to gratitude, and gratitude is linked to increase in His generosity. The generosity of Allah will not stop increasing unless the gratitude of His servant ceases."

Al-Hasan said, "Speak about His generosity frequently, for speaking about it is gratitude."

Allah commanded His Messenger, may Allah bless him

and grant him peace, to speak of His Lord's generosity in the *ayah*:

❨ And speak about the blessings of your Lord. (93:11) ❩

Allah, Exalted is He, is pleased when the effect of His generosity on His servant is made apparent, for this in itself is a form of gratitude that speaks for itself. 3

When Abu al-Mughirah used to be asked how he was, he would say, "We are immersed in the Lord's generosity, and incapable of being sufficiently grateful. He is most loving towards us, even though He does not need us, and we are disrespectful towards Him, even though we are utterly dependant on Him."

Sharih said, "Whenever a servant is afflicted with a misfortune, Allah grants him three things: that it does not affect his faith; that it is not more severe than it might have been; and that, as it was decreed, it has already happened and is over."

Yunus ibn Ubaid reported that Abu Ghunaimah was once asked, "How are you?" He replied, "I am caught between two blessings whose nature is such that I do not know which of them is more excellent: my wrong actions which Allah has concealed for me, so that no one can taunt me about them; or the affection for me which Allah has placed in the hearts of His creatures, and which, because of my actions and deeds, I do not deserve."

Suffian said about this *ayah* of the Qur'an:

❨ Leave Me (to deal) with those who reject these words. We shall gradually lead them on, in ways which they do not perceive, (68:44) ❩

that Allah makes His blessings pleasing to them, while witholding the ability to be grateful from them.

Others have said that whenever such people commit a

sin, He confers a blessing on them.

A man once asked Abu Hazim, "O Abu Hazim, what is the gratitude of the eyes?" He replied, "It is to reveal whatever good they see and to veil whatever bad they see."

The man said, "And what is the gratitude of the ears?" He replied, "If you hear something good with them you understand it, and if you hear something bad you reject it."

The man asked, "And what is the gratitude of the hands?" He said, "Do not use them to take what is not yours, and do not restrain them from giving what is due to Allah."

The man asked, "And what is the gratitude of the stomach?" He replied, "That its lower part is for food and its upper part is for knowledge," (i.e. it should not be stuffed full of food).

The man asked, "What is the gratitude of the private parts?" Abu Hazim replied by reciting the *ayat* of the Qur'an:

❨And those who guard their chastity, except with those to whom they are married, or the servants whom they own, for them there is no blame; but those whose desires exceed these limits are wrongdoers. (23:5-7) ❩

The man asked, "What is the gratitude of the feet?" He replied, "If you learn of the death of a righteous man who used to use his feet in doing good deeds and acts of worship, then use them in the same way as he did; whereas if the man who has died was someone despicable to you, then turn away from what he used to do and be grateful to Allah.

"And as for the one who uses only his tongue to express his gratitude, he is like a man who only covers himself with the hem of his garment without putting it on, so it is of no use to him in either the heat, or the cold, or the snow, or the rain."

A man of knowledge once wrote to his brother, "We have been granted so many of Allah's blessings – in spite of our many acts of disobedience – that it is impossible for us to count them. We do not know which to be most grateful for – the best of our good actions, which He enabled us to do, or the ugliest of our wrong actions which He has veiled for us."

Notes

1. Al-Bukhari, *Kitab at-Tahajjud*, 3/14; Muslim, *Kitab Sifat al-Qiyyamah*, 17/162.
2. Ahmad, *al-Musnad*, 5/245-247; al-Hakim, *Ma'rifat as-Sahabah*, 3/273; an-Nisa'i, *Kitab as-Sahw*, 3/53.
3. This is supported by a *hadith* related by at-Tirmidhi, *Kitab al-Adab*, 8/106, and by al-Hakim, *Kitab al-At'ima*, 4/135, on the authority of 'Amr ibn Shu'aib, transmitted to him by his father and grandfather, that the Prophet, may Allah bless him and grant him peace, said, "Allah likes to see the effect of His generosity on His servant." *Shaykh* Shakir classifies this *hadith* as *sahih* in his *al-Musnad*, 6708.

FIFTEEN

COMPLETE RELIANCE ON ALLAH

Complete reliance on Allah is the sincere dependence of the heart on Allah in the servant's endeavours in pursuing his interests and safeguarding himself against anything that may be harmful to his well-being both in this life and in the *akhira*:

❨ And for whoever fears Allah, He prepares a way forward for him, and He provides for him from where he does not expect. And for whoever relies on Allah, then He is enough for him. (65:2-3) ❩

A person who fears Allah and relies completely on Him, will find that these two qualities are sufficient for him both in matters of this world and of his *deen*.

Umar ibn al-Khattab, may Allah be pleased with him, said, "I heard the Messenger of Allah ﷺ say, 'If you had all relied on Allah as you should rely on Him, then He would have certainly provided for you as He provides for the birds, who wake up hungry in the morning and return with full stomachs at dusk.'" [1]

Abu Hatim ar-Razi said that this *hadith* establishes the fundamental principle that reliance on Allah is one of the most important means of acquiring one's sustenance and provision.

Sa'id ibn Jubair said, "Reliance on Allah is an essential part of faith." Possessing the state of reliance, however, does not prevent you from utilising the ways and means which Allah has decreed for His creation. These are His laws, and He has commanded us to use ways and means, while at the same time He has instructed us to rely on Him. Endeavouring to make use of the ways and means in His Universe with our limbs is obedience, and relying on Him in our hearts is faith in Him. Allah says:

❴ O you who believe, take your precautions! (4:71) ❵

Sahl said, "Whoever questions actions (e.g. striving to earn a living) questions the very validity of the *sunnah*, and whoever questions reliance on Allah questions faith itself."

Reliance is the state of the Prophet ﷺ, while striving to earn a living is his *sunnah*, and whoever behaves in accordance with the state of the Prophet ﷺ must not abandon his *sunnah*.

It has been said, "Ignoring ways and means is doubting the need for the *shari'ah* of Islam, while trusting entirely in ways and means is doubting the Reality of *Tawhid* (the existence of Allah).

There are three kinds of actions that the servant has:

First, the acts of obedience which Allah has commanded His servants to do, since He has made them the means for rescuing them from the Fire and their entering the Garden. These must be done, while at the same time still relying on Allah when doing them and seeking this outcome – for there is no strength and no power except from Him. Whatever He, the Exalted, wishes to be has already happened, and whatever He wishes not to be will never happen.

Whoever does not fulfil one of the duties which have been imposed on him by Allah deserves to be punished in this life and in the next life in accordance with the *shari'ah* and as decreed by Allah, the Exalted.

Yusuf ibn Asbat said, "Do what you do like a man who can only be saved by his actions, and rely completely on Allah like a man who can only be afflicted by the afflictions that have already been decreed for him."

Second, the actions which Allah has made a part of life in this world, and in which He has told His servants to take part – such as eating when hungry, drinking when thirsty, seeking shade in the heat, keeping warm in cold weather, and other such things. Being involved in such actions is also a duty. Whoever does not do so, to the extent that he does himself harm by abandoning them – even though he was perfectly capable of doing them – has been negligent and deserves punishment.

Third, the actions which Allah has made a part of life in general, without their being essential. Allah can make exceptions for whomever of His servants He chooses.

There are several kinds of these actions, one of which is taking medicine. The *ulama'* have given varying answers to the following question: Is it better for a sick person to take medicine or, in the case of those who rely completely on Allah, to abstain from taking it?

There are two better known answers to this question:

Imam Ahmad says that reliance on Allah for the one who has it is better. The *Imam* cites the saying of the Prophet ﷺ, "Seventy thousand people of my *Ummah* will enter the Garden without being taken to account or being punished. They are the ones who do not make talismans, or seek them, or look for omens, or treat their body by burning, and who completely rely on their Lord." [2]

Those *ulama'* who approve of taking medicine, say that the Prophet ﷺ used to take it, and he only did what was best; and that the above *hadith* only applies to the use of talismans, which are rightly regarded with suspicion because they can lead to reliance on other than Allah, and which are accordingly equated with looking for omens and treatment by burning.

Mujahid, 'Ikrimah, an-Nukha'i and several of our predecessors said, "No one has been given permission to totally abandon trying to use the ways and means of this world for treating his afflictions, except one whose heart has altogether ceased to relate to the creation."

Ishaq ibn Rahawayh was asked, "Can a man engage in warfare without making any preparation for it?" He answered, "He can, if he is like Abdullah ibn Jubair – otherwise he cannot."

Notes

1. *Sahih*, at-Tirmidhi, *Kitab az-Zuhud*, 7/8; al-Hakim, *Kitab ar-Riqaq*, 4/310.
2. Al-Bukhari, *Kitab ar-Riqaq*, 11/305; Muslim, *Kitab al-Iman*, 3/89.

SIXTEEN

LOVE OF ALLAH

Loving Allah, the Glorious, the Exalted, is the ultimate aim of all stations, and the summit of all states. Having attained the state of true love for Allah, each station that follows it is one of its fruits and a branch from its roots – such as longing, intimacy and contentment. Each station that precedes it is a step towards it – such as repentance, perseverance and doing without, or *zuhud*.

The most beneficial, the most sincere, the most elevated and the most exalted kind of love is most certainly the love of the One Whom hearts were created to love, and for Whom creation was brought into existence to adore. Allah is the One to Whom hearts turn in love, exaltation, glorification, humility, submission and worship. Such worship cannot be directed towards other than Him. It is the perfection of love accompanied by complete submission and humility. Allah, the Exalted, is loved for His own sake in every respect. All except Him are loved for the love they give in return. All the revealed Books, and the messages of all the Prophets, bear witness to the love that is due towards Him, as does the natural impulse He has created in all His servants, the intellect He has given them, and the blessings He has poured on them.

Hearts, as they mature, come to love whomever is merciful and kind towards them. So how much greater is their love for Him from Whom all kindness springs!

Every good thing enjoyed by His creation is one of His
limitless blessings, and He is One, with no associates and
no partners:

❨ And whatever good you have – it is from Allah; and
then, when misfortune comes to you, you cry to Him
for help. (16:53) ❩

And also:

❨ And from among mankind there are some who take
for themselves (objects of worship as) rivals to Allah,
loving them as they should (only) love Allah. And
those who believe are stronger in their love for Allah.
(2:165) ❩

And also:

❨ O you who believe, whoever of you becomes a rebel
against his *deen*, (know that in his place) Allah will
bring a people whom He loves and who love Him,
humble towards the believers, harsh towards the disbelievers, fighting in the way of Allah, and not fearing the
blame of anyone who blames. (5:54) ❩

The Prophet ﷺ has sworn that no servant truly believes
until he, may Allah bless him and grant him peace, is more
dear to that servant than his own child, father, and all of
mankind. [1]

The Prophet ﷺ also said to Umar ibn al-Khattab, may
Allah be pleased with him, "even until I am more dear to
you than your own self." [2]

This means that you are not a true believer until your
love for the Prophet ﷺ reaches this level.

If the Prophet ﷺ must take precedence over our own
selves[3] when it comes to what we love and what this en-
tails, then is not Allah, Exalted is He, even more deserving

of our love and adoration than our own selves?

Everything that comes from Him to His servants, whether it is something that they love or something that they hate, directs us to love of Him. His giving and His withholding, the good fortune and the misfortune that He decrees for His servants and His abasing them and elevating them, His justice and His grace, His giving life and taking it away again, His compassion, generosity and veiling of His servants' wrong actions, His forgiveness and patience, His response to His servants' supplications even though He is not in any need of His servants whatsoever – all this invites hearts to worship Him and love Him.

If a human being were to do the smallest amount of any of these things to another, that person would not be able to restrain his heart from loving him. How can a servant not love, with all his heart and body, the One Who is constantly Merciful and Generous towards him in spite of all his wrong actions?

Allah's mercy descends upon His servant from the heavens, while the servant's wrong actions rise up to him from the earth.

Allah seeks His servant's friendship and love by means of His generosity towards him, even though He is not in any need of him. The servant, on the other hand, invites Allah's anger through his disobedience and wrong actions, even though he is in need of His assistance.

Neither Allah's mercy nor His generosity towards the servant deter him from disobeying his Lord. In the same way, neither the servant's disobedience nor his wrong actions deter Allah ta'Ala from granting him His blessings.

Furthermore, while anyone whom we love and who loves us may behave like this for personal gain, Allah, Mighty and Glorious is He, does so in order to benefit us.

Furthermore, while anyone with whom we trade will not do business with us if he does not expect to make a profit from the transaction – and he will do what he can to make a profit one way or another – Allah, Mighty and Glorious is He, trades with us in order to enable us to make the best and greatest profit for ourselves from our transaction with Him. Thus one good deed counts as between ten and seven hundred good deeds, or even more, while a bad deed is recorded as only one bad deed and can be swiftly wiped out.

Furthermore, He, Glorious is He, created us for Himself and He created everything for us, both in this world and in the next. Who else, then, deserves to be loved and pleased more than Allah ta'Ala?

Furthermore, all that we – and the whole creation, for that matter – require and need is with Him. He is the Most Generous. He gives His servants more than they need, even before they ask him. He is pleased with even a little right action and increases its rewards. He forgives untold wrong actions and wipes them out. Whatever is in the heavens and the earth supplicates to Him. Everyday He is on a new affair. The multiplicity of things never bewilder Him, nor is He ever made weary by the insistent pleas of His servants. Indeed He is pleased with those who persist in their supplication.

He is pleased with those of His servants who seek His assistance, and He is angry with those who do not. He is displeased when He sees a servant being disobedient and not caring about his actions, and yet He veils His servant's wrong actions while the servant himself does not veil them. He has mercy on His servant while the servant does not have mercy on himself.

He has called him to His acceptance and mercy through His compassion and generosity – but he declines. He has sent messengers to him and made His covenant known through them. He, Glorious is He, even draws near him and says, "Is there anyone who is calling on Me, so that I may answer his prayer? Is there anyone who is seeking My forgiveness, so that I may forgive him?" [4]

How, then, can hearts not love Him, the One Who – and no one other than Him – grants rewards, answers prayers, pardons mistakes, forgives sins, veils wrong actions, dispels grief and drives away sorrow?

He alone, Exalted is He, is worthy of remembrance, gratitude, worship and praise. He is the most generous to be asked, the most liberal to give, the most merciful to pardon, the mightiest to assist and the most dependable to rely on. He is more merciful to His servant than a mother is to her baby. He is also more pleased by the repentance of the penitent sinner than a man who is overjoyed to find his riding beast with all his provisions still on its back after he had lost it in a barren land and had given up all hope of survival.

He is the King, with no partner, the One, the Unique, Who has no equal. Everything will perish except His Face. He is not obeyed unless it is by His command, nor is He disobeyed without His knowing it. He is pleased with the obedient servant for his obedience, even though it could not have occurred without His help and assistance. He pardons and forgives even after He has been disobeyed. And yet the rights which are due to Him are the ones which are most rejected and neglected.

He is the nearest witness, the most sublime protector, the most true to His Word, and the most just of all judges.

He knows the secrets of the selves. ❰ There is not an animal of whose forelock He does not have a hold. (11:57) ❱. He records the actions and decides the lifetimes of His slaves. To Him the secrets in the hearts are known and the Unseen is revealed. Everyone yearns for Him, faces humble themselves before the Light of His Face, and minds are completely incapable of understanding the Essence of His Being. All the evidence that confronts the heart and mind bears witness to the impossibility of there being anything like Him. By the Light of His Face every form of darkness has been enlightened, the heavens and the earth have been illuminated, and the whole creation has been set in order. He does not sleep, nor is it fitting for Him to do so. The actions of the night are presented before Him before daybreak, and those of the day before nightfall. He is veiled by pure light, and if the veil were to be removed, then the radiance of His Light would engulf all of His creation that His vision contains.

Love of Allah the Almighty gives life to the heart and sustains the soul. The heart experiences no pleasure, nor feels any joy, nor tastes any success – not even life – if it does not have this love. If the heart loses this love, then the loss it suffers is more severe than that of the eye when it is deprived of its sight and the ear when it is deprived of its hearing.

Even worse than this, the decay of the heart when it is devoid of love for its Creator, Source, and True God, is far worse than that of the body when it no longer contains the soul. This truth is only recognised by the people who are alive, for a wound does not pain the dead.

Fath al-Mawsili said, "The lover finds no other pleasure in life and does not neglect remembering Allah for an instant."

A righteous man once said, "The lover is always with Him: he remembers Him continually and constantly with longing, using every possible means and *nawafil* to please Him." [5]

Another man said in a poem:

And love your Lord by serving Him,
For lovers are but servants of the Beloved.

When she was giving counsel to her children, one of the women of the *Salaf* once said to them, "Make it a habit to love and obey Allah, for those who have *taqwa* take their obedience to the point where their body experiences aversion for anything other than obedience. If the cursed one (*shaytan*) tries to tempt them to do something wrong, the wrong action is ashamed and avoids them because of the way in which it is rejected by them."

Abdullah ibn al-Mubarak recited:

You disobey Allah,
and yet you still claim to love Him.
By Allah, such behaviour is disgusting,
by any standard!
You would have obeyed Him had your love been true,
For the lover is always obedient to the Beloved!

Notes

1. Al-Bukhari, *Kitab al-Iman*, 1/58; Muslim, *Kitab al-Iman*, 2/15.
2. Al-Bukhari, *Kitab al-Iman wa'n-Nudhur*, 11/523.
3. As Allah says: ❰ The Prophet is closer to the believers than their own selves. (33:6) ❱.

4. Muslim has related in his *Sahih, Kitab Salat al-Musafirin wa Qasruha,* 6/36, on the authority of Abu Huraira, may Allah be pleased with him, that the Prophet, may Allah bless him and grant him peace, said, "Our Lord, Mighty and Glorious is He, descends every night to the heaven which is nearest to us during the last third of the night and says, 'Is there anyone who is calling on Me, so that I may answer his prayer? Is there anyone who is asking of Me, so that I may grant his request? Is there anyone who is seeking My forgiveness, so that I may forgive him?'"

5. This is supported by a *hadith* related by al-Bukhari in his *Sahih,* on the authority of Abu Huraira, who said, "The Messenger of Allah, may Allah bless him and grant him peace, said, 'Allah ta'Ala has said, "Whoever displays enmity towards a friend of Mine, I shall be at war with him. My servant does not draw near to Me with anything more loved by Me than what I have made *fard* for him, and My servant continues to draw near to Me with *nawafil* until I love him – and when I love him, I am his hearing with which he hears, and his seeing with which he sees, and his hand with which he grasps, and his foot with which he walks – and if he were to ask of Me, I would surely give it to him, and if he were to ask Me for refuge, I would surely grant him it."'" Also contained in an-Nawawi, *al-Arba'in an-Nawawi, hadith* no. 38.

SEVENTEEN

CONTENTMENT WITH THE DECREE OF ALLAH

The servant may experience one of two states as regards what he dislikes: the state of being content, or that of being patient. Being content is a praiseworthy quality, while being patient is a duty which the believer must fulfil.

At some times, the people of contentment witness the Wisdom and Beauty of the One Who Tests when He tests His servant, and they see that He is always Right in whatever He decrees.

At other times, they witness the Might and Majesty and Perfection of the One Who Tests, to such an extent that they become completely immersed in these Attributes of Allah, Exalted is He, so that they do not experience any pain.

This station can only be attained by those who have great knowledge and love. And so it is possible that they find pleasure in whatever they have been afflicted with – because it has come to them from their Beloved.

The Difference between Contentment and Patience

Being patient involves restraining the self and preventing it from giving in to resentment, in spite of any suffering that it experiences – in the hope that the misfortune which afflicts it will come to an end – as well as restraining the limbs from behaving badly, out of impatience.

Being content, on the other hand, involves feeling at ease in accepting the Divine Decree, and being unconcerned with when any suffering will stop, even though it is being experienced. Being content alleviates any suffering by reason of the heart's immersion in the spirit of certainty and knowledge. If the contentment increases in its intensity, then it removes the experiencing of any suffering altogether.

It has been related on the authority of Anas ibn Malik that the Prophet ﷺ said, "When Allah loves someone then He tests him: as for whoever is content – Allah will be pleased with him; and as for whoever is discontented – Allah will be displeased with him." [1]

Ibn Mas'ud, may Allah be pleased with him, said, "Allah the Almighty has, in His Justice and Wisdom, placed refreshment and joy in certainty and contentment, and He has placed sadness and sorrow in doubt and discontentment."

When commenting on the *ayah*,

❨ No misfortune happens without the permission of Allah – and as for whoever believes in Allah, He guides his heart; and Allah Knows all things, (64:11) ❩

'Alqama said, "This concerns the misfortune which afflicts the servant: he knows that it has come from Allah, and so he comes to terms with it and feels content with it."

As regards the *ayah*,

❨ Whoever acts righteously, whether male or female, and is a believer, We will surely give him life with a good life, and We will surely give them their reward in accordance with the best of what they used to do, (16:97) ❩

Abu Mu'awiyya al-Aswar said, "'A good life' means being satisfied and content."

Ali ibn Abi Talib, may Allah be pleased with him, once saw 'Adiyy ibn Hatim looking sorrowful and so he asked him, "Why are you so sad, O 'Adiyy?" 'Adiyy replied, "How can I not be in such a state, when both of my sons have been killed and my eye gouged out?" So Ali said to him, "O 'Adiyy, whoever is content with the Decree of Allah will surely experience it and be rewarded for it; and whoever is not content with the Decree of Allah will surely experience it and Allah will make his actions worthless."

Abu'd-Darda' visited a man on his death-bed and found him praising Allah, so he said to him, "You are right! Allah, Mighty and Glorious is He, likes us to be content with whatever He decrees."

Al-Hasan al-Basri said, "Whoever is content with what he has, Allah will make it enough for him and give it blessing; and whoever is not content, Allah will neither make it enough for him nor give it blessing."

Umar ibn Abdal-Aziz said, "I have nothing that gives me any joy, except when what has been decreed by Allah happens." He was once asked, "What do you desire?" He replied, "Whatever Allah, Mighty and Glorious is He, decrees."

Abdal-Wahid ibn Zaid said, "Being content is the greatest door to Allah, the Garden of this life, and a place of rest for the worshippers."

It has also been said, "There will be no station in the *akhira* better than that of those who are content with whatever Allah decrees, at all times. Whoever enjoys the quality of contentment will be raised to the best of stations."

On discovering one morning that he had lost a great many camels, an Arab of the desert said, "By Him of Whom I am one of His slaves, were it not for some envious and malicious enemies, I would not have been pleased to see my camels still alive and in their pen – and something which Allah had decreed not taking place."

Notes

1.At-Tirmidhi, *Kitab az-Zuhud*, 7/77, classified as *hasan gharib*; as-Suyuti, *al-Jami' as-Saghir*, 2/459, classified as *hasan*.

EIGHTEEN

HOPE IN ALLAH

This is the peaceful state of a heart that awaits what is dear to it. If the means – by which what the heart awaits may come – are not present, then stupidity and folly would be more accurate descriptions of its state. If, on the other hand, what it awaits is certain to happen, then neither can certain hope be the term to use in describing its state: one cannot say, "I wish the sun would rise at sunrise", but one can say, "I wish it would rain".

Those who study the heart have taught that this world is like land which is cultivated for its fruits in the next world: that the heart is like the earth, that belief is like the seeds, and that acts of obedience are like ploughing up the soil and clearing it for planting and digging channels to bring water to it.

The heart which is in love with this world is like barren earth in which seeds cannot sprout. The Day of Resurrection is like the day of the harvest, and no one reaps what he did not sow. No seed other than the seed of belief can grow, and belief rarely brings forth any fruit if the heart is rotten and lacking morality.

In the same way that seeds do not sprout in barren earth, so a servant's hope for Allah's forgiveness can be compared to the hope of a farmer:

If anyone searches for fertile soil, sows it with good healthy seeds, supplies it with what it needs when it needs it, pulls out the weeds and anything else that might hinder or ruin the growth of the crop, and then sits waiting for Allah's blessings in the form of His keeping unfavourable weather and destructive pests away until the crop has finished growing and is ripe – then his waiting can be described as hope.

If, however, he sows the seeds in hard, barren soil which is too high up for water to reach it, and does nothing to care for the seedlings, and then sits waiting for a harvest – then his waiting can only be described as folly and stupidity, not hope.

So, the term hope only applies to waiting with longing and yearning for something to happen, after all the means which will assist in the realisation of this desire – that is, all those means which are within the servant's power and choice – have been utilised.

The things which are not within the servant's control, and which are entirely within the domain of Allah's generosity, also play a part. Allah, Exalted is He, is able to prevent all harmful phenomena and obstacles, if He so wishes.

If the servant sows the seeds of belief, and waters them with obedience to and worship of Allah, and purifies his heart of bad elements, and then waits for Allah's blessings in the form of His keeping him steady in that state until his death, and then granting him an excellent end and His forgiveness – then his waiting is truly hoping for the best.

Allah, the Exalted, says:

❨ Surely those who believe and those who make *hijra* and struggle in the way of Allah, these are the ones who have hope of the mercy of Allah; and Allah is Forgiving, Compassionate. (2:218) ❩

This means that such people are worthy of hoping for

Allah's mercy. Allah did not intend to restrict hope in Him to them alone, for others can also have hope, but He distinguishes them as the only people whose hope is really well-founded.

The one whose hope guides him to obedience of Allah and deters him from rebelling against Him has true hope; whereas the hope which leads a person on to idleness and being immersed in wrong actions is only stupidity in disguise.

It should be pointed out that anyone who hopes for something must satisfy three conditions:

First, he should hold dear what he hopes for.

Second, he should be afraid of missing it.

Third, he should strive to achieve what he hopes for.

If hope is not connected to any one of these prerequisites, then it is only wishful thinking – hope is a different matter all together.

Everyone who is hopeful is fearful. Whoever walks a path, makes haste when he fears that he may miss the goal that he hopes for.

It has been related by Abu Huraira that the Prophet, may Allah bless him and grant him peace, said, "Whoever is afraid of being plundered by the enemy sets out in the early part of the night, and whoever sets out early reaches his goal. Be on your guard! The treasures of Allah are dear and precious. Wake up! The treasure of Allah is the Garden."[1] Allah, Glorious and Exalted is He, says:

❨ Say: "O My servants who have wronged their souls, do not despair of the mercy of Allah, for surely Allah forgives all sins; surely He is Forgiving, Compassionate. (39:53) ❩

And also:

❨ And surely your Lord is full of forgiveness for mankind for their wrongdoing. (13:6) ❩

Umar ibn Abdal-Aziz reported on the authority of his father, may Allah be pleased with both of them, that the Prophet ﷺ said, " Whenever a Muslim dies, Allah casts a Jew or a Christian into the Fire in his place." [2]

It has been transmitted on the authority of Umar ibn al-Khattab, may Allah be pleased with him, that some prisoners were brought before the Messenger of Allah ﷺ. Amongst them there was a woman who was searching for someone in the crowd. When she found a baby amongst the prisoners, she took it in her arms, cradled it next to her breast, and allowed it to suckle.

Then the Messenger of Allah ﷺ said, "Do you think this woman would ever throw her child into the Fire?" We said, "By Allah, as long as it was in her power, she would never throw her child into the Fire!"

Then the Messenger of Allah ﷺ said, "Allah is more merciful to His servants than this woman is to her child." [3]

It has been related on the authority of Abu Huraira that he heard the Messenger of Allah ﷺ say, "When Allah created the creation, He decreed something for Himself, and a clear record is with Him confirming that, 'Truly, My mercy prevails over My wrath." [4]

It has been reported on the authority of Anas that he heard the Messenger of Allah ﷺ say, "Allah, Exalted is He, has said, 'O son of Adam, as long as you call on Me and ask of Me, I will forgive you for what you have done, and I shall not mind. O son of Adam, were your sins to reach the clouds of the sky and were you then to ask forgiveness of Me, I would forgive you. O son of Adam, were you to come to Me with sins nearly as great as the earth, and

were you then to face Me without having associated anything with Me, I would bring you forgiveness nearly as
great as it.'" [5]

Yahya ibn Mu'adh said, "In my opinion, the worst kind
of self-delusion is for someone to sin excessively and then
to hope for forgiveness without feeling any remorse; or it
is to expect to draw near to Allah, the Exalted, without
obeying or worshipping Him; or it is to hope for the fruits
of the Garden after having only planted the seeds for the
Fire; or it is to seek the abode of the obedient through committing wrong actions; or it is to expect a reward after having done nothing worthwhile; or it is to place hope in
Allah, Glorious and Mighty is He, after having exceeded
all the limits."

Do you hope for forgiveness when you have not trod-
den its paths? A ship does not sail on dry land. [6]

Notes

1. *Hasan,* at-Tirmidhi, *Sifat al-Qiyyama,* 7/146, classified as
hasan gharib; also al-Hakim, *Kitab ar-Raqa'iq,* 4/307.
2. Muslim, *Kitab at-Tawba,* 17/85.
3. Al-Bukhari, *Kitab al-Adab,* 10/426; Muslim, *Kitab at-Tawba,*
17/70.
4. Al-Bukhari, *Kitab Bad' al-Wahiy,* 6/287; Muslim, *Kitab at-
Tawba,* 17/68.
5. *Hasan,* at-Tirmidhi, *Kitab ad-Da'awat,* 9/524; classified as
hasan gharib.
6. Ibn Hibban has related in his book, *Rawdhat al-'Uqala',*
p.284, that the poet Abu'l-'Atahiyya said, "I went to see
Harun ar-Rashid, the commander of the faithful, and
when he saw me, he said, 'Are you Abu'l-'Atahiyya, the
poet?' I said, 'Yes.' Then he said to me, 'Give me some

counsel in a few lines of poetry, and be brief!' I recited to him:

> Do not feel secure from death at any time:
> Even if you seek protection
> in your advisers and your guards,
> know that the arrows of death
> are always pointing in our direction,
> whatever armour and shields we may have.
> Do you hope for forgiveness
> when you have not trodden its paths?
> A ship does not sail on dry land."

NINETEEN

FEAR OF ALLAH

Fear is the spur with which Allah urges His servants to-wards knowledge and action so that they can draw nearer to Him. It is the pain and anguish of the heart when it senses that harm is imminent. Fear is what restrains the body from being disobedient and compels it to worship and service. When fear is lacking, this leads to negligence and boldness in committing sins, whereas too much fear results in a state of hopelessness and despair.

Fear of Allah, Exalted is He, sometimes springs from knowledge of Him, and of His Attributes – the knowledge that it would be of little concern to Him to obliterate the heavens and the earth, and that nothing can stop Him from doing so if He so wishes.

At other times it is caused by the enormity of the wrong actions which the servant commits.

At other times it is caused by a combination of all these things: the degree of a servant's fear depends on his awareness of his own faults, and on his awareness of Allah's Glory, Might and Self-Sufficiency – and of the fact that He is not accountable for what He does, while His servants are.

The person who fears His Lord most is the one who has most knowledge of Him and of himself. This is why the Prophet ﷺ said, "By Allah, of all people, I am the one with the most knowledge of Allah, and I fear Him the most." [1]

Imam ash-Sha'bi was once addressed as, "O knowledge-able one." He replied, "I am not – for the knowledgeable one is the one who fears Allah, as He, Mighty and Glorious is He, says:

❨ Surely those of His servants who know fear Allah. (35:28) ❩ "

Those Who Fear Allah

The one who experiences fear is not the one who weeps and wipes his eyes, but the one who abandons whatever may bring punishment upon him. Dhu'n-Nun al-Misri was once asked, "When is a servant really afraid?" He replied, "When he is in the same state as a sick man who seeks protection in Allah out of fear that his sickness will be prolonged."

Abu'l-Qassim al-Hakeem said, "Whoever fears something runs away from it, while whoever fears Allah runs towards Him." Al-Fudayl ibn 'Iyyad said, "If you are asked whether you fear Allah, do not reply; for if you say 'Yes', you would be lying, and if you say 'No', it would mean that you do not believe in Him."

Fear burns up forbidden desires, and the wrong actions which can be so dear to a servant soon become distasteful, just as honey becomes repugnant to someone who desires it, if he discovers that it is poisoned. Fear tames the limbs and fills the heart with submission, humility and tranquillity. Arrogance, hatred and envy depart from it, and it is filled with Him, through fear of Him and through contemplating the danger of His punishment – and so it becomes occupied with nothing other than Him, and has no concern other than contemplation, bringing itself to account and striving in the way of Allah.

A servant with such a heart becomes watchful over every breath and every moment, and constantly reprimands the self for its inner thoughts, its actions and its words. His state is like that of a person who is trapped in the claws of a lion, not knowing whether it will leave him alone and allow him to escape, or whether it will attack him and kill him. Thus he becomes both inwardly and outwardly occupied with what he fears. There is no room in him for anything other than what he fears. This is the state of a person who is overwhelmed by fear of Allah.

The Merits of Fear of Allah

Allah, Mighty and Glorious is He, grants guidance, mercy, knowledge and acceptance to those who fear Him:

❦ Guidance and mercy for those who fear their Lord. (7:154) ❧

And also:

❦ Surely those of His servants who know fear Allah. (35:28) ❧

And also:

❦ Their reward is with their Lord: Gardens of Eden underneath which rivers flow wherein they will dwell for ever; Allah is pleased with them, and they are pleased with Him; this is for whoever fears his Lord. (98:8) ❧

Allah has commanded His servants to fear Him and has made belief conditional upon fear. He, Glorious and Mighty is He, says:

❦ Fear Me if you are believers. (3:175) ❧

This is why it is inconceivable that a believer can be devoid of fear of Allah, however slight it may be. The weakness of his fear is in proportion to the weakness of his knowledge and faith.

The Prophet ﷺ said, "No believer who has wept from fear of Allah, Exalted is He, will ever enter the Fire unless milk returns back into its udder." [2]

Al-Fudayl ibn 'Iyyad said, "Whoever fears Allah will be guided by this fear to all good."

Ash-Shibli said, "There was never a time that I feared Allah without my finding a door of wisdom and guidance opening up to Him." Yahya ibn Mu'adh said, "Any wrong action committed by a believer is followed by two consequences: fear of punishment and hope for forgiveness." Allah, the Exalted, says in the Qur'an:

❲ Surely those who live in awe out of fear of their Lord, and those who believe in the signs of their Lord, and those who do not associate partners with their Lord in their worship, and those who give what they give with fear in their hearts because they are returning to their Lord – it is these who hasten to do good, and in this they are foremost. (23:57-61) ❳

It has been reported by Aisha, may Allah be pleased with her, that she said, "I asked the Messenger of Allah ﷺ about these *ayat*, saying, 'Are they those who drink intoxicants, and commit adultery and steal?' He, may Allah bless him and grant him peace, said, 'No, O daughter of as-Sideeq,[3] it is those who regularly fast and pray and give *zakat* and fear that their good deeds may not be accepted: ❲ it is these who hasten to do good. ❳'" [4]

It has been related on the authority of Abu Dharr, may Allah be pleased with him, that the Messenger of Allah ﷺ recited the *surah* from the Qur'an beginning with the *ayah*:

❴ Has there ever been any period of time for man in which he was something not remembered? (76:1) ❵

Then he ﷺ said, "I see what you do not see and I hear what you do not hear. Heaven has groaned and it has a right to groan. By Him in Whose hand my soul is, there is not a space of even four fingers width in which there is not an angel who prostrates his forehead before Allah. I swear by Allah that if you knew what I know, you would laugh little and weep much, and you would not take delight in women, but you would go out to an open space and call on Allah for help. I wish I were a tree that could be cut down and cease to exist." 5

This *hadith* indicates that if we knew as much as the Prophet ﷺ knew about the Might of Allah, and His retribution for whoever disobeys Him, then our weeping and grief and fear for what might await us would be long lasting. We might never laugh at all.

Aisha, may Allah be pleased with her, reported that whenever the wind changed and storms blew, the Prophet's ﷺ demeanour would change and he would walk to and fro in the room in agitation, going out and then coming back in again. All of this was out of fear of Allah's punishment. 6

Abdullah ibn ash-Shukhair related that whenever the Messenger of Allah ﷺ started doing the prayer, a sound like a bubbling cauldron could be heard coming from his chest. 7

If you consider the state of the companions of the Holy Prophet ﷺ, and the righteous men of this *Ummah* who succeeded them, may Allah be pleased with all of them, you will find that they were fully involved in doing the best of deeds while, at the same time, they were full of fear of Allah. We, on the other hand, all do things which fall far short of this example, and yet feel quite secure.

Abu Bakr as-Siddiq, may Allah be pleased with him, said, "I wish I were no more than a hair on the side of a believing servant." Whenever he got up to do the prayer, he would be trembling like a leaf out of fear of Allah.

Umar ibn al-Khattab, may Allah be pleased with him, was once reading *Surat at-Tur* and when he came to the *ayah*:

❴ Surely the doom of your Lord will indeed come to pass. (52:7) ❵,

and he wept so intensely that he fell ill, so that people came to see how he was.

When he was on his death bed he told his son, "Put my cheek next to the earth so that Allah may forgive me." Then he said, "I am doomed if He does not forgive me." He repeated the same words three times and then he died.

When he used to recite the Qur'an at night and read an *ayah* that filled him with fear, he would stay indoors for days on end so that people would come to visit him, thinking that he was ill. His frequent weeping etched two dark lines on his face.

Ibn Abbas once told him, "Allah has brought many countries into the Muslim *Ummah* through you, and through you many a victory has been won." Umar replied, "All I hope for is to be saved. I desire neither reward nor punishment."

Uthman ibn Affan, may Allah be pleased with him, used to cry until his beard was soaked each time that he stood at a grave. He used to say, "If I were standing between the Garden and the Fire, not knowing in which one of the two I would end up, I would rather be turned into ashes before I learned of my fate."

Abu'd-Darda' used to say, "If you knew what you will encounter after your death, you would never eat with any appetite, nor drink thirstily, nor enter houses to shelter, but you would go out into open spaces and beat your breast and weep at your lot. I wish I were a tree to be cut up and destroyed." [8]

Ibn Abbas had skin under his eyes which looked like worn out sandal leather, due to his frequent weeping.

Ali ibn Abi Talib, may Allah honour him, was once overwhelmed with sadness after completing the dawn prayer; he said, "Never before did I see anything like the companions of the Messenger of Allah ﷺ. Their hair was dishevelled, their faces were pale, they were covered in dust, and the space between their eyes looked like the knees of goats. They had spent the night in prayer and recitation of the Qur'an, either on their feet or in prostration. When the dawn came, they would spend it in remembrance of Allah, swaying like trees on a stormy day, with tears streaming from their eyes until their clothes were soaked. By Allah, it seems to me that the people who are around me now have passed the night fast asleep." Then he got up and was never seen laughing again, until he was stabbed to death by Ibn Muljim.

Musa ibn Mas'ud said, "Whenever we sat in the company of Suffian, we would feel as if the Fire had surrounded us because of the fear and panic we could see in his eyes." Al-Hasan was once described as follows: "Whenever he approached us, it would seem as if he had only just returned from the burial of his best friend; whenever he sat in a company, he would be like a prisoner who has just been sentenced to death by having his head cut off;

and whenever the Fire was mentioned, it would be as if it had been created especially for him."

It has been related that Zurarah ibn Abu Awfa led some people in the dawn prayer and recited *Surat al-Mudathir* from the Qur'an. When he reached the words:

❮ For when the trumpet shall sound, that will be –
that Day – a Day of Distress, (74:8-9) ❯,

he gasped and fell down dead. [9]

Abdullah ibn Amr ibn al-As is reported to have said, "Weep, and if you cannot weep, then pretend to weep! I swear by Him in Whose hand my life is that if any of you really knew, you would plead until your voice went, and pray until your back was broken." [10]

Notes

1. Al-Bukhari, *Kitab al-Adab*, 10/513; Muslim, *Kitab al-Fadha'il*, 15/106; on the authority of Aisha, may Allah be pleased with her.
2. *Sahih*, at-Tirmidhi, *Kitab Fadha'il al-Jihad*, 5/260 and *Kitab az-Zuhud*, 6/600; classified as a *sahih hadith*.
3. 'As-Sideeq' – meaning 'the truthful one' – is a name that was given to Aisha's father, Abu Bakr, may Allah be pleased with both of them, because of his honesty, truthfulness and going straight – and because he always confirmed the truth of the Prophet's message and of his words and actions, may Allah bless him and grant him peace.
4. *Sahih*, at-Tirmidhi, *Kitab at-Tafsir*, 9/19; al-Hakim, *Kitab at-Tafsir*, 2/393.
5. *Sahih*, al-Bukhari, *Kitab ar-Riqaq*, 11/319; at-Tirmidhi, *Kitab az-Zuhud*, 6/601.

6. Al-Bukhari, *Kitab Bad' al-Khalq*, 6/300; Muslim, *Kitab al-Istisqa'*, 6/196.

7. *Sahih*, at-Tirmidhi, *Kitab ash-Shama'il*, p.337; an-Nisa'i, *Kitab as-Sahw*, 3/13; Abu Daw'ud, *Kitab as-Salah*, 3/172.

8. *Da'if*; this *hadith* is not only ascribed to Abu'd-Darda', but is also recorded by as-Suyuti, *al-Jami' as-Saghir*, 3/318, as a *hadith* related by Ibn 'Asakir. Al-Hakim records a similar *hadith* but with different wording in *al-Mustadrak*, 4/579, and ascribes it to Abu'd-Darda'.

9. Ad-Dhahabi, *Kitab al-'Ibar*, 1/109.

10. *Sahih*, al-Hakim, *Kitab al-Ahwaal*, 4/578.

TWENTY

THE LIFE OF THIS WORLD

The disapproval of this world that appears in the Book
and the Hadith is not directed at its time aspect, which is
the alternation of night and day until the Day of
Judgement. Allah, the Mighty and Glorious, has provided
them so that people who wish to do so can invoke His
Name and be thankful during them.

It was once said, "The night and the day are like two
treasure-chests, so be careful of what you do in them."
Mujahid said, "Not a day passes which does not say, 'O
son of Adam, I have come to you today and I will never
come again, so be careful of what you do during my stay.'
When the day has passed, it is folded up and sealed, never
to be reopened by anyone until Allah reopens it on the
Day of Judgement." There is a poem that goes:

Life is nothing other than a road
that leads to the Garden,
or to the Fire.
Its nights are a man's workshop,
and its days are his market place.

So time is the servant's capital.

The Prophet ﷺ said, "Whoever says, 'Exalted is Allah
and His are the Blessings', will have a palm tree planted
for him in the Garden." [1]

Consider how many palm trees a time waster misses the opportunity of planting. A righteous man used to say to his guests who stayed too long, "Don't you want to leave? The angel of the sun never tires of pulling it." A man once told an *'alim*, "Stop, so that I can talk to you!" The *'alim* replied, "First stop the sun!"

The disapproval of this world that appears in the Book and the Hadith is not directed at its space aspect either, which is the earth and all its mountains, and seas, and rivers, and the treasures within it. All these are Allah's blessings for His servants, so that they can make use of them, and contemplate them and thereby recognise the Oneness and Greatness of their Maker, Exalted is He. The disapproval is directed at the actions of the sons of Adam in this world, most of which do not have any good consequences; for as the Glorious and Exalted says:

❨ Know that the life of this world is only playing about and idle talk and showing off and boasting amongst yourselves, and competing in wealth and children. It is like a crop after rain whose growth pleases the farmer – but then it dries up, and you see it turn yellow, and then it becomes straw. (57:20) ❩

In this life, the sons of Adam are divided into two types: The **first** type denies the existence of an abode which awaits Allah's servants after this life is over, where reward and punishment are experienced. These are the ones about whom Allah says:

❨ Surely those who do not look forward to their meeting with Us, but are pleased with the life of this world and feel secure in it, and those who do not pay attention to Our signs – their abode will be the Fire, because of what they used to earn. (10:7-8) ❩

Such people have only one concern, which is to enjoy life and pursue all its pleasures – and the Exalted says:

❴ And those who reject take it easy and eat like cattle eat – and the Fire will be their abode. (47:12) ❵

The **second** type are those who accept that there is an abode after death, where there is both reward and punishment. These are the ones who follow the Messengers. They fall into three categories: those who are unjust to themselves, those who are mean to themselves, and those who are swift in doing good deeds, by the will of Allah.

First, those who are unjust to themselves form the majority. Most of them are content with the blossoms of this life and its pleasures, helping themselves to them and using them in ways which Allah has not commanded. The world appears to them to be their greatest concern, and with it they are satisfied; they only love and hate for its sake.

These are the people who play about and chatter and are diverted by the attractions of this world. Although they may believe in the *akhira* in a general way, they have not discovered what this life is meant for, nor are they aware that it is only a stopping place where provisions for the final journey can be acquired.

Second, those who are mean to themselves are those who take what is permitted from this world and fulfil their duties in it, but who then pursue what lies beyond these duties for the sake of their own pleasure and in order to enjoy the delights of this world.

Such people will not be punished for doing so, but their pleasure seeking will result in their rank being diminished.

Umar ibn Al-Khattab, may Allah be pleased with him, said, "If it had not been for the fact that my station in the

Garden might be diminished, I would have imitated you in your life of ease; but Allah has warned some people by saying:

❴ You squandered the good things that you had in the life of the world, and you sought contentment in them. (46:20) ❵"

Third, those who are swift in doing good deeds are the ones who understand what this world is meant for, and they act accordingly. They know that Allah has only put His servants in this world in order to see which of them have the best actions:

❴ Surely We have put what is on the earth as a glittering show so that We may test them, as to which of them have the best actions. (18:7) ❵

This means that Allah has put what is on the earth in order to test us, to see who is going to avoid the pleasures of this world and look for success in the next world, for:

❴ And surely We shall turn what is on it into a heap of dust. (18:8) ❵

Those who race to do good deeds only take from this world whatever provisions are necessary for the journey. The Messenger of Allah ﷺ said, "What have I to do with this world? As regards this world, I am like a rider who rests under the shade of a tree, and then continues his journey and leaves it." ²

The Prophet ﷺ also told ibn Umar, "Be in this life as if you were a stranger or a wayfarer." ³

Whenever the intention behind taking pleasure in what is *halal* is the obedience and worship of Allah, then the enjoyment of such pleasures is regarded as an act of obedience for which the servant is rewarded.

As Mu'adh ibn Jabal, may Allah be pleased with him, said, "I look forward to Allah's reward for the time which I spend asleep, just as I look forward to it for the time which I spend awake." [4]

Sa'id ibn Jubair said, "The provisions of arrogance and pride are what distract you from the *akhira*. The provisions that do not distract you are the ones which you need – in order to reach what is better than the provisions themselves."

Yahya ibn Mu'adh said, "How can I not love this world in which I have been blessed with sustenance that gives me life, when I use this life for worship by means of which I can earn the reward of the Garden?"

Abu Safwan ar-Ra'ini was once asked, "What is the life of this world which is criticised in the Qur'an, and which those who are prudent should avoid?" He replied, "Everything that you do in this world with the intention of making a profit in this world is blameworthy, and everything that you do in order to profit in the next world has nothing to do with this world."

Al-Hasan said, "How sweet and good the life of this world is for the *mumin* – for without having to make too much effort, he takes his provision from it for the Garden; and how awful the life of this world is for the *kafir* and the *munafiq* – for they waste their nights and they take their provision from it for the Fire!"

Abu Musa related that the Prophet ﷺ said, "Whoever is in love with his life in this world damages his life in the next world, and whoever is in love with his life in the next world damages his life in this world – and you should prefer what lasts for ever to what is destined to vanish." [5]

Awn ibn Abdullah said, "This life and the next life hang in the balance in the heart as if on scales. Whichever

142 The Purification of the Soul

one predominates, the other becomes lighter and less significant." Wahab said, "This life and the next life are like a man with two wives. If he pleases one he incurs the wrath of the other."

Abu'd-Darda said, "If you swear to me that a certain man is the most God-fearing amongst you, I will swear to you that he is the best amongst you."

Abdullah ibn Mas'ud addressed some people saying, "You have undertaken more good actions than the companions of the Messenger of Allah ﷺ ever did, but they are still better than you are because they turned away from worldly pleasures and gains." [6]

The Harm in Love for this World

Imam Ahmad wrote, on the authority of Suffian, that Jesus the son of Mary, peace be on them, used to say, "Love for this world is the root of all evil, and having money is a serious illness." He was asked, "What ill effects does it have?" He replied, "Whoever has it is never safe from pride and self-delusion." They said, "What if someone is safe from these defects?" He said, "His being preoccupied with doing good will distract him from the remembrance of Allah, Glorious and Mighty is He." [7]

Love for this world is what fills the Fire, while doing without the pleasures of this world is what fills the Garden. Being intoxicated with love for this world is more disastrous than being intoxicated by alcohol, because a person who is drunk with this world only finally comes to his senses in the darkness of his grave.

Yahya ibn Muadh said, "The life of this world is the wine of *shaytan*, and whoever is intoxicated by it only wakes up once he is amongst the hordes of the dead, lamenting among the losers."

The least of its evils is that it distracts man from the remembrance and love of Allah. Whoever is distracted by his wealth is a loser. If the heart is distracted from the remembrance of Allah, then *shaytan* takes up residence in it and directs it towards whatever he wishes. When *shaytan* makes a heart familiar with the ways of evil, he prompts it to do a few good deeds in order to delude its owner into thinking that he is, on the whole, a doer of good.

Ibn Mas'ud said, "Each and every person in this world is like a guest and his wealth is only on loan. The guest leaves and the loan is eventually repaid." [8]

It has been said that love for the life of this world is the root of all evils, for it ruins people's faith in so many ways:

First, love for it leads to over-emphasising its importance – when it is insignificant in the sight of Allah. It is one of the greatest wrong actions to attach importance to what Allah considers trivial.

Second, Allah has condemned it. He dislikes and disapproves of it, except for whatever it contains that is duly His. Whoever loves what Allah condemns, dislikes and disapproves of, has left himself open to confusion and temptation, as well as to His disapproval and anger.

Third, a person who loves this world makes the pleasures and achievements of this life his goal. In order to acquire them he will utilise the very ways and means which in fact Allah has provided for him in order to lead to Him and to the *akhira*. Such a person rebels against what Allah intended him to strive to achieve: he makes the means an end in itself, and uses the means that should lead to the *akhira* to acquire the pleasures of this world.

This is a complete perversion of what these means were intended for, which indicates a most perverted heart. Allah, the Most Exalted, says:

❰ As for whoever desires the life of this world and its glitter, We shall repay them for what they did in it, and in this they will not be wronged. These are the ones for whom there is nothing in the next world but the Fire; whatever they attempt in it is in vain, and everything they used to do is wasted. (11:15-17) ❱

There are many *ahadith* to this effect. One of them was transmitted by Abu Huraira who said, "I heard the Messenger of Allah, may Allah bless him and grant him peace, say, 'The first of men to be judged on the Day of Judgement will be a man who died as a martyr. He will be brought forward and Allah will ask him to recount His blessings, and so he will recount them. Allah will say, "What did you used to do?" The man will say, "I fought for You until I died a martyr." Allah will say, "You have told a lie. You fought so that you would be called a brave warrior, and so you were called." Orders will be given against him and he will be dragged face downwards and thrown into the Fire.

'Then a man will be brought forward who acquired knowledge and passed it on, and who recited the Qur'an. He will be brought before Allah Who will ask him to recount His blessings, and so he will recount them. Then Allah will ask, "What did you used to do?" He will say, "I acquired knowledge and passed it on, and I recited the Qur'an, seeking Your pleasure." Allah will say, "You have told a lie. You acquired knowledge so that you would be called a scholar, and you recited the Qur'an so that it might be said that you were a *qari*, and so you were called." Then orders will be given against him and he will be dragged face downwards and thrown into the Fire.

'Then a man will be brought forward whom Allah had made abundantly rich and to whom He had granted every kind of wealth. He will be brought forward and Allah will ask him to recount his blessings, and so he will recount them. Then Allah will ask, "What did you used to do?" He will say, "I spent money in every way in which You wished it to be spent." Allah will say, "You are lying. You did this so that it might be said that you were a generous man, and so it was said." Then Allah will give the order and he will be dragged face downwards and thrown into the Fire.'" [9]

In this *hadith* we can see how it was love for the life of this world that deprived these three people of reward and rendered their actions worthless, making them the first to enter the Fire.

Fourth, love for the life of this world also makes the servant become preoccupied with it and prevents him from undertaking actions which would benefit him in the next world. There are many different kinds of people in this category: there are those whose preoccupation with this life distracts them from Islam and its laws altogether; those who are distracted from many of their religious duties; those who are distracted from any duty that hinders their plans and schemes to acquire it; those who are distracted from fulfilling their religious obligations at the right times and in the right manner, thereby wasting their time and neglecting their duties; those whose hearts are too preoccupied with this life to be able to give their full attention to their worship when they fulfil their religious duties; and those whose hearts are not devoted to Allah, so that their fulfilling these duties is only an outward show without any inward sincerity – and these are the least common type from amongst the lovers of this life.

A less extreme form of love for the life of this world is that in which it simply distracts the servant from his true source of happiness: which is to dedicate his heart to the love of his Lord, and his tongue to remembering Him. Love for and obsession with the life of this world inevitably limit the servant's chances in the next world, in the same way that love for the next world limits his life in this world.

Fifth, love for the life of this world makes it the servant's chief preoccupation. Anas ibn Malik, may Allah be pleased with him, reported that the Messenger of Allah ﷺ said, "Whoever is preoccupied with the next life, Allah will place his wealth within his heart, and gather his people around him, so that life will come and offer itself to him. Whoever is preoccupied with this life, Allah will make his poverty apparent in his eyes, and scatter his people from around him, and only what has been written for him in this world will come to him." [10]

Sixth, the one who loves the life of this world the most is the one who suffers from it the most. His suffering is of three kinds: his suffering in this life itself as a result of his striving to achieve worldly gains and his competing with its people over them; his suffering in the *barzakh* because he missed out in this life and regrets his lost opportunities – for now he is on his way to meet Allah in such a state that he wishes he will never meet Him; and his suffering because he did not succeed in finding a substitute for Him in this life. Such a man suffers the most severe torment in the grave as sorrow, grief and regret all eat away at his soul, just in the same way as the worms who are eating away at his body.

To summarise, the one who loves the life of this world suffers in this world, in his grave, and on the Day that he meets his Lord. Allah, the Most Exalted, says:

❨ So do not let their wealth and their children dazzle you. Surely Allah intends to punish them in the life of this world through this, and they themselves will perish while they are disbelievers. (9:55) ❩

One of our righteous predecessors said about this *ayah*, "Allah 'punishes them' through their striving to acquire this world; 'they will perish' as a result of their love for it; 'while they are disbelievers' because they have denied the rights which are due to Allah in it."

Seventh, the one who loves the life of this world and prefers it to the next life is the lowest of creation and the least intelligent: he prefers illusion to reality, dreaming to being wide awake, the short-lived shade to eternal bliss, and the temp-orary shelter to the everlasting abode. He exchanges his life in the *akhira* for one which is no more than an illusion. A life that is no more than a passing shadow cannot fool any Muslim who has an intellect.

Some of our predecessors have often quoted this verse of poetry:

O people who take pleasure
in a world that will vanish,
falling in love
with a fading shadow
is sheer stupidity!

Yunus ibn Abdal-'Ala said, "To me the life of this world can be compared to a man who falls asleep, and in a dream he sees whatever he likes and whatever he dislikes, and while he is in this state, he suddenly wakes up!"

One of the things to which this life can most easily be compared is a shadow: it appears to be permanent, but in reality it is in a constant state of growing smaller or larger, and when you try to chase it and catch it – you cannot! It can also be compared to a mirage in a desert which:

❨ The thirsty one imagines is water until he reaches it and finds that it is nothing and instead of it he finds Allah Who pays him what is due to him – and Allah is swift in the reckoning. (24:39) ❩

The life of this world can also be compared to a deformed, repulsive, old woman who is untrue and deceitful to whomever proposes to her. She dresses in all manner of adornment and beautiful attire in order to conceal her ugliness and fickleness. Her suitors, deceived by her outward appearance, eventually propose to her.

She tells them, "I want no dowry from you – except that you give up the *akhira*: I and the *akhira* are deadly enemies, and we are neither permitted nor allowed to meet each other."

The suitors, completely taken in by her words, reply, "There is no blame on those who must unite with their beloved."

When, however, they lift her veil, and her disguise is revealed, they find themselves in all sorts of difficulties. Some of them divorce her and free themselves from the burden, while others on the other hand, decide to remain with her – only to end up, on the morning after the wedding, sad and sorrowful.

By Allah! Her invitation invites the whole world to hurry and come not to success, but to failure – and yet her admirers seek union with her day and night. They rush to join her in the darkness, only to awake the next morning demoralised and with their hopes shattered.

They fall right into her trap, and she consigns them to their fate.

Notes

1. *Sahih*, at-Tirmidhi.
2. *Sahih*, at-Tirmidhi, *Kitab az-Zuhud*, 7/48; al-Hakim, *Kitab ar-Riqaq*, 4/310; on the authority of Abdullah ibn Mas'ud and of Umar, may Allah be pleased with them.
3. *Sahih*, al-Bukhari.
4. *Sahih*, Muslim, *Kitab al-Imaara*, 12/207; and ascribed to Mu'adh.
5. *Da'if*, Ahmad ibn Hanbal, al-Musnad, 4/412; al-Hakim, *Kitab ar-Riqaq*, 4/308; it is classified as *sahih*, but adh-Dhahabi rejected it due to its having a break in its *isnad*.
6. Abu Nu'aym, *al-Hilya*, 1/136.
7. *Da'if*, see *Majmu'at al-Fatawa*, 18/123.
8. A verse of poetry with the same meaning says:

> Your wealth and your family
> are only with you on trust,
> And whatever is held on trust
> must inevitably be returned.

9. Muslim, *Kitab al-Jihad*, 13/50.
10. *Sahih*, at-Tirmidhi, *Kitab az-Zuhud*, 6/165; Ibn Ma'jah, *Kitab az-Zuhud*, 2/1375.

TWENTY-ONE

REPENTANCE

Turning away from wrong actions by turning to the Concealer of faults and the Knower of all secrets is the basis of those who travel to Him, the initial investment of those who finally profit, the first step in the quest for His Face, the key to putting right whatever is not correct, and the primary stage in the selection of those who will be brought close to Him.

The station of turning in repentance is at the beginning, in the middle, and at the end. The servant who seeks Him never abandons it. He remains in it until his death. If he moves on to another station, he takes it with him and arrives with it. Turning in repentance is the beginning of the servant and his end. Allah, the Most Exalted, says:

❨ And turn to Allah altogether, O you who believe, so that you may succeed. (24:31) ❩

This *ayah* is in a Madinan *surah* in which Allah addresses the people of *iman* and those who have been honoured from amongst His creation. He called upon them to turn in repentance to Him after they had already believed, made *hijra*, and fought *jihad*. Then He made success conditional on repentance, using the word 'may' in order to make the believers aware that they could only hope for success if they turned to Him in repentance, may Allah make us follow in their footsteps. Allah says:

❴ And those who do not turn in repentance are indeed wrongdoers. (49:11) ❵

He distinguishes between servants who are repentant and those who are wrongdoers, and makes no other distinction. He calls those who do not turn in repentance, wrongdoers and transgressors, and says that no one is more of a wrongdoer than such a person, because of his ignorance of his Lord and of the rights that are due to Him, as well as because of his own faults and the harmfulness of his actions.

The Prophet ﷺ said, "O people, turn in repentance to Allah! I swear by Allah that I turn in repentance to Him more than seventy times each day." [1]

Repentance is the servant's turning to Allah and his turning away from the company of those who stray away from the straight path and those who invite Allah's anger.

There are three conditions for repentance to be valid if the wrong action is to do with what is due to Allah, Exalted and Glorious is He: feeling regret, abandoning the wrong action, and resolving never to repeat it again.

Repentance is invalid without regret because if there is no regret for having done something wrong, then this implies that it is considered acceptable, as well as being alright to do again. The Prophet ﷺ said, "Feeling regret is a part of repentance." [2]

Abandoning the wrong action is crucial, because repentance is meaningless if the bad deed continues to be committed.

The third condition, resolving never to repeat the wrong action again, depends in essence on the sincerity of this resolve and its honesty. Some *ulama'* have said that repeating the wrong action nullifies the repentance, arguing that if someone who has repented returns to the wrong action, whenever that may occur, then this shows that his repentance was false and therefore invalid. The majority, however, conclude that this is not necessarily a condition.

If the wrong action was committed against a fellow human being, then the one who repents must either put right whatever damage he has caused or make amends to the person whose rights he has infringed. The Prophet 🅼 said, "Any one of you who is indebted to his brother in Islam must settle his debt today, before the time comes when there will be no money, and only good deeds and bad deeds will count." [3]

This kind of wrong action is a transgression against two parties, each of whom have their own particular rights. The wrongdoer shows his repentance by paying his fellow human being his due, and by paying what is due to Allah by inwardly regretting his wrong action. This regret is a private matter, between him and his Creator.

There are a number of particular types of repentance, of which we mention the following:

First, the repentance for back-biting or slander, where the question arises as to whether the person who has been maligned in his absence should be informed of the repentance of the wrongdoer, and so consequently come to know about a wrong of which he would otherwise have remained oblivious.

Both the *madhdhahib* of *Imam* Abu Hanifa and *Imam* Malik make informing the person who has been maligned a precondition for the validity of the repentance. They rest their argument on the above mentioned *hadith*.

The other opinion, which is that of Ibn Taimiyya, does not consider this necessary. Instead, he judges that it is enough for the wrongdoer to repent in private to Allah, and to speak of the person whom he has slandered in the same company as the one in which he had previously maligned him, but this time in terms which are the opposite of those which originally caused the trouble; and he must also ask Allah to forgive him.

His argument is that if the person who has been maligned is told about it, then this brings the wrong to his attention, and only causes more trouble without achieving any good. Allah does not make precipitating such a state of affairs permissible, let alone make it compulsory or command us to act like this.

Second, the repentance for stealing money must include the return of that money to its rightful owners. If the one who repents does not know to whom the money belongs, or if it is not possible for the money to be returned for any other reason, then he must give away the equivalent in charity on their behalf.

On the Day of Judgement they will have the choice of either approving of his action – in which case the reward for the charity goes to them – or of disapproving of it and having whatever they are entitled to in it from his reward – in which case the reward for the charity goes to the one who repented, for Allah never annuls the reward for charity.

It has been related that Ibn Mas'ud, may Allah be pleased with him, once bought a woman slave from a man. When he went to pay him, he found that the man had disappeared. Ibn Mas'ud waited in vain for the man to return, and eventually gave the money away in charity, saying, "O Allah, this *sadaqa* is on that man's behalf. If he approves of this *sadaqa* then its reward is his, and if he does not, then the reward is mine and he receives a reward equal to my reward."

Third, what is the position of someone who receives payment for doing something *haram*, such as selling alcohol, singing, or making a false testimony, and who then repents while the payment is still in his possession?

One group of the *ulama'* say that he should return the payment to whomever gave it to him, since it still belongs to the one who made the payment because the transaction was not *halal* and it did not result in any *halal* reward from Allah.

Another group of the *ulama'* say – and this judgement is more correct – that his repentance can only be valid if he gives away the payment in charity, for how can he return money which was spent in being disobedient to Allah?

The same principal applies to someone whose *halal* and *haram* money become so mixed up that he is no longer able to distinguish between the two: he should give away in charity whatever amount he thinks is *haram*, and purify what is left. Allah knows best.

Another question is this:

When a servant turns in repentance for a wrong action, does he return to the station in which he was before he committed that wrong action?

One group of the *ulama'* say that he does return to the same station he was in before committing the wrong action, because repentance wipes away the wrong action completely, and it becomes as if it had never taken place.

Another group say that he does not return to the same station, arguing that since he had been moving forward before committing the wrong action, and since committing it made him go backwards, then when he repents he loses the equivalent of the distance that he could have covered in the meantime, had he not committed the wrong action!

Ibn Taimiyya said, "The correct judgement is that some of those who repent do not return to their former station, while others move on to an even higher station and become better than they were before they committed the wrong action."

For example, the Prophet Daw'ud, peace be on him, was in a better station after he had turned in repentance than he was in before he committed his wrong action.

Here is a metaphor to shed more light on the matter:

A traveller was making his way, feeling confident and safe, walking a while and then running a while, and then resting or sleeping. He came across a shady place, with abundant cool water and a blossoming garden, and decided to rest for a while. While he was relaxing, he was attacked by an enemy who seized him and tied him up. He saw destruction looming and thought that his end had come, that he would become a feast for lions and never reach his destination.

While he was in this state, troubled by thoughts of despair, his merciful and caring father suddenly appeared before him. He untied him and told him to be on his way and to be wary of the enemy which lurked in ambush along the road. He assured him that as long as he remained alert and vigilant he would not be overcome, but that if he was negligent he would once again be captured.

His father said that he would go ahead and lead him to his destination. If the traveller stayed alert and kept his presence of mind and remained prepared for his enemy, then his journey would be better than it had been before, and he would arrive more quickly. If, on the other hand, he forgot about his enemy and returned to his former state of inattention and forgetfulness, indifferent to danger and only mindful of the pleasant garden, then he would once again become an easy target.

Sincere Repentance

Allah, Glorious and Mighty is He, says:

❮ O you who believe, turn to Allah with sincere repentance so that your Lord may free you from your bad deeds and bring you into Gardens underneath which rivers flow, on the Day when Allah will not disgrace the Prophet and those who believe with him. (66:8) ❯

For repentance to be true and sincere it must be free from deceit, defects and corruption. Al-Hasan al-Basri said, "It is when the servant regrets what has happened and resolves never to repeat it again." Al-Kalbi said, "It is when the servant asks for forgiveness with his tongue, feels regret in his heart, and restrains his limbs." Sa'id ibn al-Musayyib said, "Sincere repentance is what you purify your souls with."

Ibn al-Qayyim said, "Being sincere in turning in repentance consists of three things: it must include all the wrong actions of the one who is repenting, leaving none of them aside; it must be accompanied by complete truthfulness and resolve, so that the one who repents does not hesitate or delay, but summons up all his will and determination and embarks upon it wholeheartedly; and it must be free of any impurities and faults that might taint its sincerity, so that it is inspired by fear of Allah, hope for what He has, and dread for whatever punishment He might inflict – and not by any desire to safeguard his possessions, or his family, or his social status, or his influence, or to attract people's praise or escape their blame, or to avoid being bothered by nuisances, or to satisfy his appetite for life, or because of his bankruptcy or inability to cope, or any other such ills that would affect the validity of his repentance and his sincerity towards Allah, Mighty and Exalted is He.

"The first element of sincere repentance concerns the action for which the repentance is made. The second concerns the person who repents himself. The third concerns the One to Whom he repents.

"The sincerity of the repentance means that it is true and includes all wrong actions. There is no doubt that such turning in repentance requires, and includes, seeking forgiveness, and that it leads to all of the sins that have been committed being wiped out. It is a most excellent and perfect repentance." [4]

A servant's sincere turning in repentance to Allah is guaranteed both with forgiveness from Allah even before it takes place, and with forgiveness from Him after it is completed. In other words, the servant turns in repentance between two acts of forgiveness from Allah which secure his salvation. Allah's first act of forgiveness is a permission, an inspiration and a means of assistance which lead to the servant's turning in repentance – which then in turn results in more forgiveness from Allah. The second act of forgiveness is one of acceptance and recompense. Allah, Mighty and Glorious is He, says:

❰ (He also turned in mercy) to the three who were left behind, when the earth, for all its spaciousness, seemed narrow to them, and their own selves were constricted for them, until they realised that there is no escape from Allah except to Him. Then He turned to them in forgiveness, so that they could turn to Him in repentance; surely Allah is Relenting, Compassionate. (9:118) ❱

Here, Allah, Exalted is He, informs us that His turning to them in forgiveness preceded their turning to Him in repentance, and that it was this that made it possible for them to turn in repentance in the first place. He was the cause of their turning in repentance – which is part of the secret of why He is called *'al-Awwal wa 'l-Akir'* – 'the First and the Last'. It is He Who makes things possible and helps to make them happen; the cause is from Him and the consequence is from Him.

The servant is oft-repentant and Allah is oft-Forgiving. The repentance of the servant is his turning back to His Lord after his having turned away. The forgiveness of Allah is of two kinds, one being permission and assistance, and the other being acceptance and reward.

Repentance has a beginning and an end:

Its beginning is turning to Allah by taking the straight path which He has commanded His servants to follow:

❴ And surely this is My straight path so follow it; and do not follow any (other) paths, lest you are separated from His path. (6:153) ❵

Its end is to return to Him on the Day that has already been decreed by taking the path which He has commanded, and which leads to His Garden. Whoever turns in repentance to Allah in this life, Allah will turn to him and reward him at the appointed Time:

❴ Whoever turns in repentance and does good has truly turned to Allah in true repentance. (25:71) ❵

The Subtle and Hidden Aspects of Repentance

If a sensible servant happens to commit a wrong action, there are a number of things he should take into account:

First, he should consider Allah's commands and prohibitions and conclude that it was a wrong action and admit that he has done it.

Second, he should consider Allah's promises and warnings which will arouse fear in him and make him turn in repentance.

Third, he should consider the fact that Allah has given him the possibility and the ability to turn in repentance, when He could have prevented him from doing wrong in the first place.

This gives him some insight into the nature of Allah – His Names, His Attributes, His wisdom, His mercy, His tolerance and His generosity. This gives him a quality of worship of Allah which he could never have possessed had he remained ignorant of these matters. The servant recognises the relationship between Allah's Creation and His promises and His warnings and His Names and His Attributes, and sees that this relationship requires these Names and Attributes, and their manifestation in the Creation.

This insight opens the servant up to such gardens of knowledge, and faith, and the secrets of the decree, and wisdom, that the domain of words is too limited to encompass and express them.

Some of what can be said is that the servant learns about Allah's Might, which is manifested in His decree – that is, that He, Exalted and Mighty is He, decrees whatever He wishes. He also learns that through the perfection of His Might, He has decreed that the servant's heart must turn, and will be directed towards whatever He wishes, and that He comes between the servant and his own heart.

By recognising some of the manifestations of Allah's Might that are made apparent through His decree, he sees that he is part of an ordered, patterned creation, the control of which is in hands that are not his own. He is only safe when Allah safeguards him, and he is only successful when Allah gives him success. He is unimportant and insignificant, in the hands of the Mighty, the Praiseworthy.

By gaining insight into the Might manifested through His decree, the servant witnesses the fact that all perfection, praise and might is Allah's, and that it is he himself who is the one with all the shortcomings and blameworthy qualities, full of faults, imperfections and needs. The more he perceives his own insignificance and his defects and weaknesses, the more he witnesses Allah's might and wealth and the more aware he is that Allah alone is perfect.

The servant learns that Allah, Exalted is He, conceals the wrong action when it is committed even though He is all-Seeing and perfectly able, if He so wishes, to expose it. In recognising that Allah gives time to the wrong doer – even though He could have been swift in punishment had He so wished – Allah's forbearance is revealed to the one who turns in repentance, and he gains an insight into the meanings of His Name, *'al-Haleem'* – 'the Forbearing'.

The servant becomes acquainted with Allah's gift of forgiveness. It is a blessing from Him. When He judges with severity, He is Just and Praise-Worthy, but His forgiveness arises out of His mercy, and the servant is not entitled to it as of right. This means that the servant should be grateful to Him, and love Him and turn to Him in repentance, recognising and relying on His Name, *'al-Ghaffar'* – 'the Often-Forgiving'.

Allah leads His servant through the stations of humility, submission, surrender and expressing his need for assistance – which are in four stages: the humility that arises out of need and poverty, which is a general attribute of all creatures; the humility of obedience and of submission, which only belongs to those who obey Him; the humility of love, for the lover is especially humble, and the degree of his humility is in direct proportion to his love; and the humility that arises as a result of disobedience and wrong action which are themselves a consequence of the poverty and need in which they result.

When all four stages are complete, humility before Allah and and submission to Him is complete and perfect. The servant realises that Allah's Name, *'ar-Razzaq'* – 'the Sustainer' necessitates what is sustained, and that His Names, *'as-Samee', al-Baseer'* – 'the all-Hearing, the all-Seeing', necessitate what is seen and heard.

In the same way, His Names, *'al-Ghafur, al-Afu', at-Tawwab'* – 'the Forgiving, the Effacer of wrong actions, the One Who Relents and Turns in Forgiveness', necessitate someone whom Allah forgives, and whose wrong actions are effaced, and who is forgiven again and again. It is impossible for the servant to ignore the implications and requirements of these Names and Attributes.

This was pointed out by the most knowledgeable of all in the creation of Allah, His Messenger ﷺ, when he said, "If you did not have wrong actions, Allah would remove you and replace you with a people who did have wrong actions, so that they could seek Allah's forgiveness and He could grant them His forgiveness." [5]

Anas ibn Malik al-Ansari reported that the Messenger of Allah ﷺ said, "Allah is more pleased with the repentance of His servant than a person riding a camel in a waterless desert who loses his camel and all his provisions of food and drink which it is carrying. Having abandoned all hope of ever finding the camel, he lies down in the shade of a tree that he happens to come across. While he is rest-ing, he suddenly sees the camel standing right in front of him. He grasps hold of its reins and then, in sheer joy, blurts out, 'O Lord, You are my Servant and I am Your lord!' He makes this mistake out of extreme joy." [6]

Let us assume that a person whom you love dearly has been captured by an enemy and prevented from joining you, and you know that this enemy will inflict all manner of tortures on your beloved and destroy him, and that you are far better for him than this enemy – for he is someone whom you have nurtured.

Then imagine that he escapes from this enemy and comes to you without letting you know in advance, so that you are amazed to find him at your front door, praising you, and hoping for your pleasure, with his cheeks smudged with the dust from your door step. How happy would you be at his return, seeing that you had already made him yours before, approved of his closeness to you, and favoured him above everyone else?

That is the feeling that you experience – even though it was not you who brought him into existence and granted him your blessings. Allah, Mighty and Glorious is He, is the One who brought His servant into existence, created him, and granted him His blessings – and He likes to com-plete His blessings on him!

Our final wish is that you do not forget to ask Allah for us to have truthfulness, sincerity, certainty, forgiveness, and health in this world and in the next world. We ask Allah that we will be among those whose final *du'a* is:

All praise is for Allah, the Lord of the worlds.

Yours is the Glory, our Lord, and to You all praise belongs. I bear witness that there is no god but You, and I seek Your forgiveness and I turn in repentance to You.

Notes

1. *Sahih*, al-Bukhari, *Kitab ad-Da'awaat*, 11/101.
2. *Sahih*, Ahmad ibn Hanbal, *al-Musnad*, 1/376, on the authority of Ibn Mas'ud. *Shaykh* Shakir says that its *isnad* is *sahih*. Also reported by al-Hakim, *al-Mustadrak*, 4/243.
3. Al-Bukhari, *Kitab al-Madhalim*, 5/101 and *Kitab ar-Riqaq*, 11/395, on the authority of Abu Huraira.
4. Ibn al-Qayyim, *Madarij as-Salikin*, 1/310.
5. Muslim, *Kitab adh-Dhikr wa'd-Du'a*, 17/65.
6. Al-Bukhari, *Kitab ad-Da'awat*, 11/102; Muslim, *Kitab adh-Dhikr wa'd-Du'a*, 17/63, on the authority of Anas, may Allah be pleased with him.

GLOSSARY OF ARABIC TERMS

Allah – ta'Ala: Allah – the Most High, the Lord of all the worlds. Allah, the supreme and mighty Name, indicates the One, the Creator, the Worshipped, the Lord of the Universe.

adhan: the call to prayer.

ahadith: the plural of *hadith*.

ahlu'l-sunnah wa'l-jama'a: the people who follow the *sunnah* of the Prophet Muhammad, may Allah bless him and grant him peace, and who hold together as a community on that basis; the body of the Muslim community.

akhira: the next world, what is on the other side of death, the world after this world in the realm of the Unseen; it is not the life in the *barzakh*, but the life either in the *jannah* or in the *nar*.

'alim: a man of knowledge from amongst the Muslims who acts on what he knows.

'aqidah: belief or faith firmly based on how things are, rather than on how they may be imagined. Thus *'aqidah* can only fully be derived from an original revelation from Allah and from the teaching of the Messenger to whom it was revealed: in this age, the Qur'an and the Prophet Muhammad, may Allah bless him and grant him peace.

Arafat: a plain fifteen miles to the east of Makka on which stands the *Jebel ar-Rahma* – 'the Mount of Mercy'. One of the essential rites of the *hajj* is to stand on Arafat, on or near the *Jebel ar-Rahma*, between mid-afternoon and sunset on the 9th of *Dhu'l-Hijjah*, making *du'a*.

arwah: the plural of *ruh*.

ayah: a sign, a verse of the Qur'an.

ayat: the plural of *ayah*.

bara': withdrawing from and opposing all that is displeasing to Allah and His Messenger, may Allah bless him and grant him peace.

baraka: a blessing, any good which is bestowed by Allah, and especially that which increases; a subtle beneficent spiritual energy which can flow through things and people or places. Purity permits its flow, for it is purity itself, which is light. Density of perception blocks it. It is transformative, healing and immeasurable.

barzakh: an interspace between two realities which both separates and yet links them; commonly used to describe the interspace between the *dunya* and the *akhira*, which begins when death takes place, when the *ruh* leaves the body – and ends when the Last Day arrives, when the *ruh* and the body are reunited again.

bid'a: innovation, changing the original teaching of the Prophet Muhammad, may Allah bless him and grant him peace, in any way.

da'if: weak; a category of *hadith* which is the opposite of that which is *sahih*.

dawa: inviting or calling people to worship Allah by following his Messenger, Muhammad, may Allah bless him and grant him peace, and his teaching, the way of Islam.

deen: the life-transaction, submission and obedience to a particular system of rules and practices, a debt of exchange between two parties, in this usage between the Creator and the created. Allah says in the Qur'an: **Surely the *deen* with Allah is Islam.** (3.19).

dhikru'llah: remembrance of Allah, invocation of Allah. All *'ibada* is dhikru'llah.

dinar: gold coinage, approximately 4.5 grams of gold.

dirham: silver coinage, approximately 3.00 grams of silver.

du'a: making supplication to Allah, asking Allah for whatever you desire.

dunya: the world, not as a cosmic phenomenon but as it is experienced; this world as opposed to the *akhira*.

fajr: dawn, first light, and in particular the time of the obligatory dawn prayer, also known as *subh*.

faqih: a man learned in knowledge of *fiqh* who by virtue of his knowledge can give a legal judgement.

fard: obligatory, an obligatory act of worship or practice of the *deen* as defined by the *shari'ah*. This is divided into *fardun'ala'l-ayan* which is what is obligatory for every adult Muslim, and *fardun'ala'l-kifaya* which is what is obligatory for at least one of the adults in any Muslim community.

fiqh: the science of the application of the *shari'ah*.

fuqaha: the plural of *faqih*.

ghusl: ritual washing of the whole body with water alone in order to be pure for the prayer.

hadith: reported speech, particularly of, or about, the Prophet Muhammad, may Allah bless him and grant him peace.

hadith qudsi: those words of Allah on the tongue of His Prophet, may Allah bless him and grant him peace, which are not part of the Revelation of the Qur'an.

hajj: the annual pilgrimage to Makka which every Muslim who has the means and ability must make once in his or her life-time; the performance of the rites of the *hajj* in the protected area which surrounds the Ka'aba. The *hajj* is one of the indispensable pillars of Islam.

halal: permitted by the *shari'ah*.

haqiqah: truth, reality.

haram: forbidden by the *shari'ah*; also a protected area, an inviolable place or object.

hasan: good; a category of *hadith* which is reliable, and therefore acceptable, but which is not as well authenticated as one which is *sahih*.

hijra: emigration in the way of Allah. Islam takes its dating from the *hijra* of the Prophet Muhammad, may Allah bless him and grant him peace, from Makka to Madina, in 622 A.D.

'ibada: any act of worship.

'id: a festival; there are two main *'Ids* in the Muslim year – the *'Id al-Adha* which seals the rites of the *hajj*, and the *'Id al-Fitr* which marks the end of the fast of Ramadan.

ihram: the conditions of clothing and behaviour adopted by someone on *hajj* or *umrah*.

ihsan: the state of being absolutely sincere to Allah in oneself; it is to worship Allah as though you see Him, knowing that although you do not see Him, He sees you.

imam: the one who leads the prayer, an eminent scholar.

iman: acceptance, belief, trust in Allah. *Iman* is to believe in Allah, His angels, His revealed Books, His messengers, the Last Day, the Garden and the Fire, and that everything is by the Decree of Allah, both the good of it and the bad of it.

iqama: the call which announces that the *fard* prayer is just about to begin.

'isha: night, and in particular the obligatory night prayer.

Islam: peace and submission to the will of Allah, the way of life embodied by all the prophets, given its final form in the prophetic guidance brought by the Prophet Muhammad, may Allah bless him and grant him peace. The five pillars of Islam are the affirmation of the *shahada*, doing the *salat*, paying the *zakat*, fasting the month of *Ramadan*, and doing the *hajj* once in a life-time if you are able.

isnad: the record, either memorised or recorded in writing, of the names of the people who form the chain of human transmission, person to person, by means of which a *hadith* is preserved – and accordingly these people themselves. One of the sciences of the Muslims which was developed after the Prophet Muhammad's death, may Allah bless him and grant him peace, is the science of assessing the authenticity of a *hadith* by assessing the reliability of its *isnad*.

jahiliyyah: the time of ignorance, before the coming of Islam.

jama'a: the main body of the Muslim community; also, in the context of doing the *fard* prayers, any body of Muslims who do a *fard* prayer together, usually in a mosque, as opposed to doing it singly, often elsewhere.

jannah: the Garden, Paradise, the final destination and resting place of the *muminun* in the *akhira*.

jihad: struggle, particularly fighting in the way of Allah, to establish and defend Islam. Inwardly, the *jihad* is to oppose whatever in your self is displeasing to Allah. Outwardly, it is to oppose *kufr* by word and action.

jinn: unseen beings created from smokeless fire who co-habit the earth together with mankind.

Ka'aba: the cube-shaped building at the centre of the *Haram* in Makka, originally built by the Prophet Ibrahim, peace be on him, and rebuilt with the help of the Prophet Muhammad, may Allah bless him and grant him peace; also known as the House of Allah. The Ka'aba is the focal point which all Muslims face when doing the *salat*. This does not mean that Allah lives inside the Ka'aba, nor does it mean that the Muslims worship the Ka'aba. It is Allah Who is worshipped and Allah is not contained or confined in any form or place or time or concept.

kafir: a person who commits *kufr*, an unbeliever, one who covers up the true nature of existence, the opposite of a *mumin*.

kafirun: the plural of *kafir*.

kalima: the declaration, **There is no god but Allah, Muhammad is the Messenger of Allah,** may Allah bless him and grant him peace.

khutbah: a speech, and in particular a standing speech, given by the *Imam* before the *jumu'a* prayer and after the two *'Id* prayers.

kufr: to cover up the truth, to reject Allah and His Messenger, may the blessings and peace of Allah be on him.

la ilaha illa'llah: there is no god but Allah.

madhdhab: a school of *fiqh*, particularly those deriving from the four great scholars of Islam: *Imam* Malik, *Imam* Abu Hanifa, *Imam* Shafi', and *Imam* Ibn Hanbal.

madhdhahib: the plural of *madhdhab*.

Madina: the city, often called *al-Madina al-Munawarra* – the illuminated, or the enlightened, city – where the revelation of the Qur'an was completed and in which the Prophet Muhammad died and is buried, may Allah bless him and grant him peace.

Makka: the city in which the Ka'aba stands, and in which the Prophet Muhammad was born, may Allah bless him and grant him peace, and where the revelation of the Qur'an commenced.

makruh: disapproved of, without being forbidden, by the *shari'ah*.

marfu': a *hadith* from a companion of the Prophet Muhammad containing words attributed to the Prophet Muhammad, may Allah bless him and grant him peace.

Muhammad ar-Rasulu'llah: Muhammad is the Messenger of Allah, may Allah bless him and grant him peace.

muhsin: someone who possesses the quality of *ihsan*.

mumin: a believer, someone who possesses the quality of *iman*, who trusts in Allah and accepts His Messenger, may Allah bless him and grant him peace.

muminun: the plural of *mumin*.

munafiq: a hypocrite; the hypocrites amongst the Muslims outwardly profess Islam on the tongue, but inwardly reject Allah and His Messenger, may Allah bless him and grant him peace, siding with the *kafirun* against the Muslims. The deepest part of the Fire is reserved for the *munafiqun*.

munafiqun: the plural of *munafiq*.

mushrik: one who commits *shirk*.

mushrikin: the plural of *mushrik*.

muslim: someone who follows the way of Islam, doing what is obligatory, avoiding what is forbidden, keeping within the limits prescribed by Allah, and following the *sunnah* of the Prophet Muhammad, may Allah bless him and grant him peace, in what he or she is able. A Muslim is, by definition, one who is safe and sound, at peace in this world, and promised the Garden in the next world.

nafl: a gift, from the same root as *anfal*, meaning booty taken in war; it means a voluntary act of *'ibada*.

nafs: the illusory experiencing self.

nar: the Fire of *Jahannam*, Hell, the final destination and place of torment of the *kafirun* and the *munafiqun* in the *akhira*.

nawafil: the plural of *nafl*.

nifaq: hypocrisy.

nufus: the plural of *nafs*.

qadar: the decree of Allah, which determines every sub-atomic particle in existence, and accordingly whatever appears to be in existence. One of Allah's Names is *'al-Qadir'* – 'the Powerful, the One Who does what He wants, the One Who has Power over everything'. The Prophet Muhammad, may Allah bless him and grant him peace, said, "Everything is by decree." (*Al-Muwatta* of *Imam Malik*: 46.1.5).

qadi: a judge, qualified to judge all matters in accordance with the *shari'ah*.

qari: one who recites the Qur'an, constantly and correctly.

qiblah: the direction faced in prayer, which, for the Muslims, is towards the Ka'aba in Makka.

Qur'an: the 'Recitation', the last Revelation from Allah to mankind and the *jinn* before the end of the world, revealed to the Prophet Muhammad, may Allah bless him and grant him peace, through the angel Jibril, over a period of twenty-three years, the first thirteen of which were spent in Makka and the last ten of which were spent in Madina. The Qur'an amends, encompasses, expands, surpasses and abrogates all the earlier revelations revealed to the earlier messengers, peace be on all of them. The Qur'an is the greatest miracle given to the Prophet Muhammad by Allah, for he was illiterate and could neither read nor write. The Qur'an is the uncreated word of Allah. The Qur'an still exists today exactly as it was originally revealed, without any alteration or change or addition or deletion. Whoever recites the Qur'an with courtesy and sincerity receives knowledge and wisdom, for it is the well of wisdom in this age.

rak'a: a unit of the prayer, a complete series of standing, bowing, prostrations and sittings.

rak'at: the plural of *rak'a.*

Ramadan: the month of fasting, the ninth month in the Muslim lunar calendar, during which all adult Muslims who are in good health fast from the first light of dawn until sunset each day. The Qur'an was first revealed in the month of Ramadan. The fast of Ramadan is one of the indispensable pillars of Islam.

ruh: the spirit which gives life; also the angel Jibril.

sadaqa: giving in the way of Allah, a gift to another or others without any motive other than the giving.

sahaba: companions, particularly the companions of the Prophet Muhammad, who learned the *deen* of Islam directly from him, may the blessings and peace of Allah be on him and on his family and on his companions.

sahih: healthy and sound with no defects; often used to describe a fully authenticated *hadith*.

sajdah: the act of making prostration, particularly in the prayer.

salafi: adjective from *as-salaf*, 'the early years', and used generally to describe the early generations of the Muslims, particularly the *sahaba*, the companions of the Messenger of Allah, may the blessings and peace of Allah be on him and on his family and on his companions, and their immediate followers. In the present age the term is used to describe those Muslims who closely follow the *sunnah* of the Prophet Muhammad.

salat: the prayer, particularly the five daily obligatory ritual prayers of the Muslims which are called *maghrib*, *'isha, fajr, dhur* and *'asr*. They consist of fixed numbers of *rak'ai* in worship to Allah. *Salat* is one of the indispensable pillars of Islam.

sawm: fasting, particularly the fast of Ramadan, from food and drink – and making love if you are married – during daylight, from the first light of dawn until sunset.

shahada: to witness, to bear witness that: **There is no god but Allah** and that **Muhammad is the Messenger of Allah,** may Allah bless him and grant him peace. The *shahada* is the gateway to Islam in this world and the gateway to the Garden in the next world. It is easy to say, but to act on it is a vast undertaking which has far-reaching consequences, both in inward awareness and in outward action, both in this world and in the next world. The *shahada* is one of the indispensable pillars of Islam.

shari'ah: a road, the legal and social modality of a people based on the revelation of their prophet. The last *shari'ah* in history is that of Islam. It abrogates all previous *shari'ahs*. It is, being the last, the easiest to follow, for it is applicable to the whole human race wherever they are.

shaykh: an old man, an *'alim* who has knowledge of Allah and of His Messenger, may Allah bless him and grant him peace, and of the *deen* of Islam.

shaytan: a devil, particularly Iblis (Satan), an evil *jinn* who prompts mankind and the *jinn* to rebel against Allah. *Shaytan* is part of the creation of Allah, and we seek refuge in Allah from the evil that He has created.

shirk: the unforgiveable wrong action of worshipping something or someone other than Allah or associating something or someone as a partner with Him; the opposite of *Tawhid* which is affirmation of Divine Unity. *Shirk* is idol-worship, which is attributing form to Allah by attempting to confine Him within an object, a concept, a ritual or a myth – whereas Allah is not like anything and has no form. He cannot be conceived of or perceived.

sirah: the historical study of the Prophet Muhammad's life, may the blessings and peace of Allah be on him.

sunnah: a form, the customary practice of a person or group of people. It has come to refer almost exclusively to the practice of the Messenger of Allah, Muhammad, may Allah bless him and grant him peace, but also comprises the customs of the first generation of Muslims in Madina, who acted in accordance with what they had learned from him and who transmitted what they had learned to the next generation. The *sunnah* is a complete behavioural science that has been systematically kept outside the learning framework of this society, but which nevertheless has been preserved by those to whom it has been transmitted and who continue to embody it as their way of life. The Messenger of Allah said: "I have left two matters with you. As long as you hold to them, you will not go the wrong way. They are the Book of Allah and the Sunnah of His Prophet." (*Al-Muwatta* of *Imam* Malik, 46.1.3).

surah: a form, a chapter of the Qur'an, composed of *ayat* linked by thematic content.

tafsir: commentary and explanation of the Qur'an.

taqwa: being careful, knowing your place in the cosmos. Its proof is the experience of awe of Allah, which inspires a person to be on guard against wrong action and eager for actions which are pleasing to Him.

taslim: giving the Muslim greeting of '*As-salaamu-alaikum*' – 'Peace be on you'. The *salat* ends with a *taslim*.

tawba: returning to correct action after error, turning away from wrong action to Allah and asking His Forgiveness, turning to face the Real whereas before one turned one's back. Your turning to Him is in reality His turning to you.

Tawhid: the Divine Unity, Unity in its most profound sense. Allah is One in His Essence and His Attributes and His Acts.

'ulama: the plural of *'alim.*

Ummah: the body of the Muslims as one distinct and integrated community or nation.

umrah: the lesser pilgrimage to the Ka'aba in Makka and the performance of its rites in the protected area which surrounds the Ka'aba. You can go on *umrah* at any time of the year.

wala': loyalty, holding fast to all that is pleasing to Allah and His Messenger, may Allah bless him and grant him peace. Whoever possesses *al-wala' wa'l-bara'* loves with the love of Allah and hates with the hate of Allah.

witr: a single *rak'a* which makes uneven the number of *sunnah* prayers done between *'isha* and *fajr*. It can be prayed at any time after *'isha* and before *fajr*.

wudu: ritual washing of the hands, mouth, nostrils, face, forearms, head, ears and feet with water alone so as to be pure for the prayer.

Yawm al-Qiyama: the Day of Standing – the Last Day – when everyone who has ever lived will be given life again, their actions and intentions in this world weighed in the balance, and their final abode determined; also known as *'Yawm al-Ba'ath'* – the Day of Rising, *'Yawm al-Hashr'* – the Day of Gathering, *'Yawm al-Qiyama'* – the Day of Standing, *'Yawm al-Mizan'* – the Day of the Balance, *'Yawm al-Hisab'* – the Day of Reckoning, *'Yawm ad-Deen'* – the Day of the Life-Transaction, and *'Yawm al-Akhira'* – the Day of the Next World. The Last Day will be followed by eternity, either in the Garden or in the Fire, for ever.

zahid: the one who practices *zuhud*, someone whose heart is not attached to the pleasures and distractions of the life of this world.

zakat: the wealth tax obligatory on Muslims each year, usually payable in the form of one fortieth of surplus wealth which is more than a certain fixed minimum amount, which is called the *nisab*. *Zakat* is payable on accumulated wealth, especially gold and silver, merchandise, certain crops, certain livestock, and on subterranean and mineral wealth. As soon as it is collected it is redistributed to those in need, as defined in the Qur'an and the *hadith*. *Zakat* is one of the indispensable pillars of Islam.

zakat al-fitr: a small obligatory head-tax imposed on every responsible Muslim who has the means for himself and his dependants. It is paid once yearly near the end of Ramadan just before the *'Id al-Fitr*.

zuhud: doing without what you do not need and making do with little.

Other Publications by Al-Firdous Ltd

The Present Rulers and Islam

Al-Wala' wa'l-Bara'

Forthcoming Publications

Alliance with non-Muslims

Jihad, the Forgotten Obligation

Jihad, the Way to Victory

The Tafsir of Ibn Kathir

Al-Wala' wa'l-Bara' - Part Two

Al-Amr bi'l-Ma'rouf wa'l-Nahi
'an'l-Munkar of Imam Ibn Taymiyah

Enquiries

Al-Firdous Ltd.,
96 Bedford Hill,
Balham,
London SW12

Ta-ha Publishers Ltd.,
1 Wynne Road.
London SW9
Tel: 0171 737 7266

SINCERE REPENTANCE

Imam Abu Hamid Ghazali
Imam Ibn Qayim Jawziya
Imam Ibn Rajab Hanbali

وَسَبِّحْ بِحَمْدِ رَبِّكَ قَبْلَ طُلُوعِ الشَّمْسِ وَقَبْلَ غُرُوبِهَا

طه : من الآية ١٣٠

Al-Firdous Ltd, London

FEAR OF ALLAH

in the light of the Quran, the Sunnah and the predecessors

Imam Ghazali, Imam Ibn Qayyim and Ibn Rajab Hanbali

Al-Firdous Ltd, London

TAQWA:
THE PROVISION OF BELIEVERS

IMAM GHAZALI
IMAM IBN QAYYIM
IBN RAJAB
HANBALI

بسم الله الرحمن الرحيم

مخضرة ... الأرض فتصبح ... السماء ... أنزل من ... الله ... أن ترى ... ألم

سورة الحج ـ الآية ٦٣

Al-Firdous Ltd, London